This book belongs to

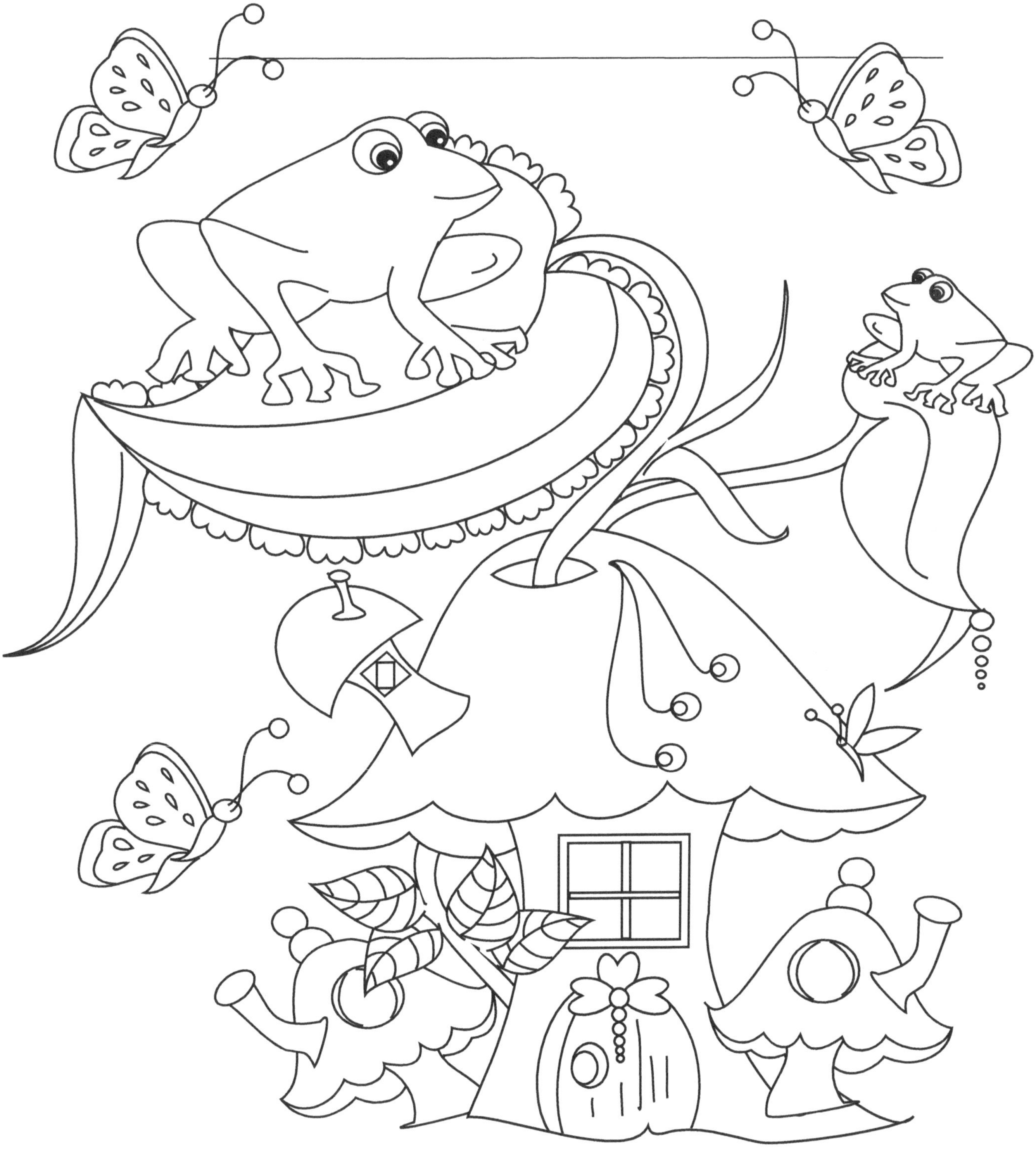

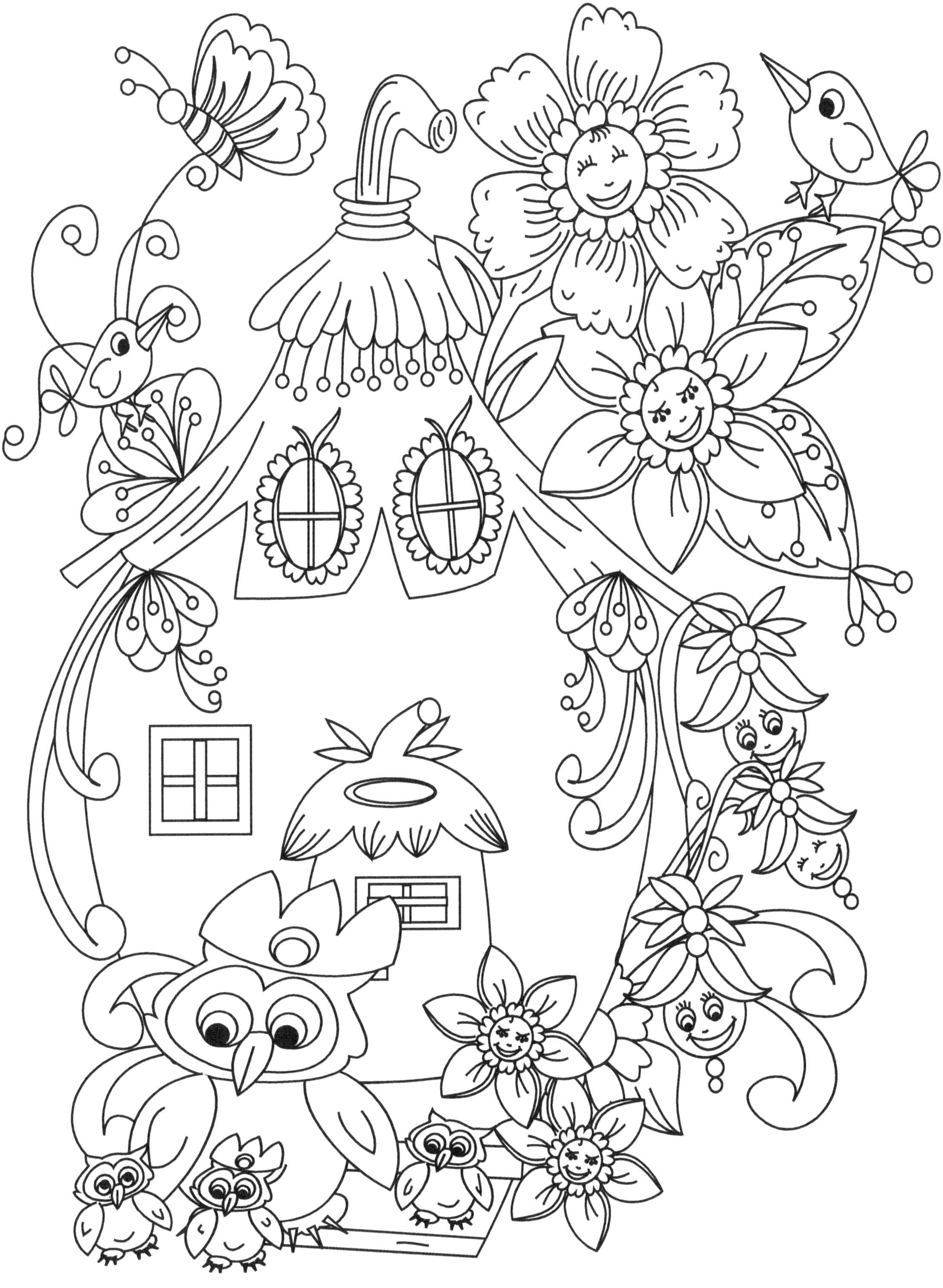

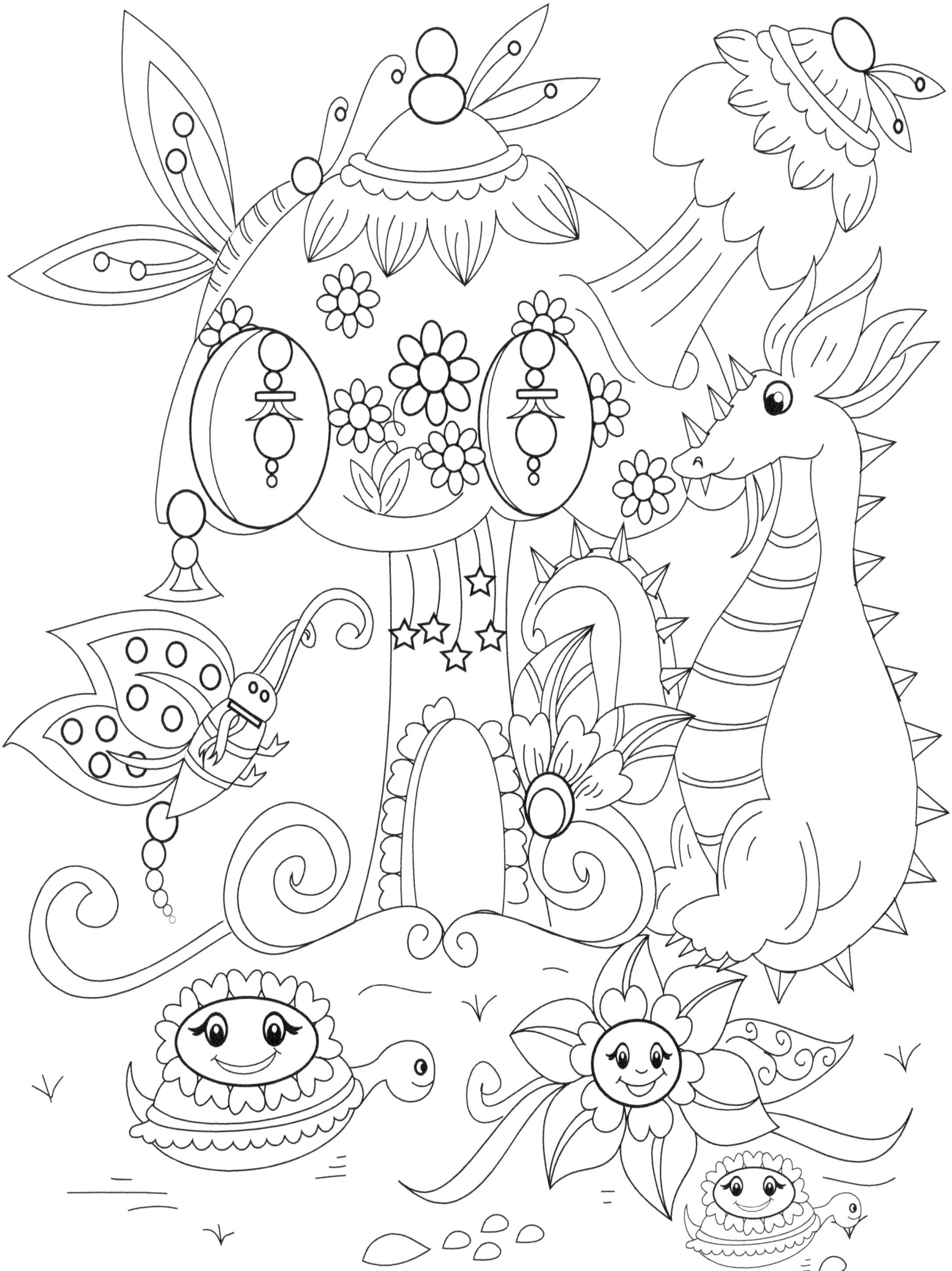

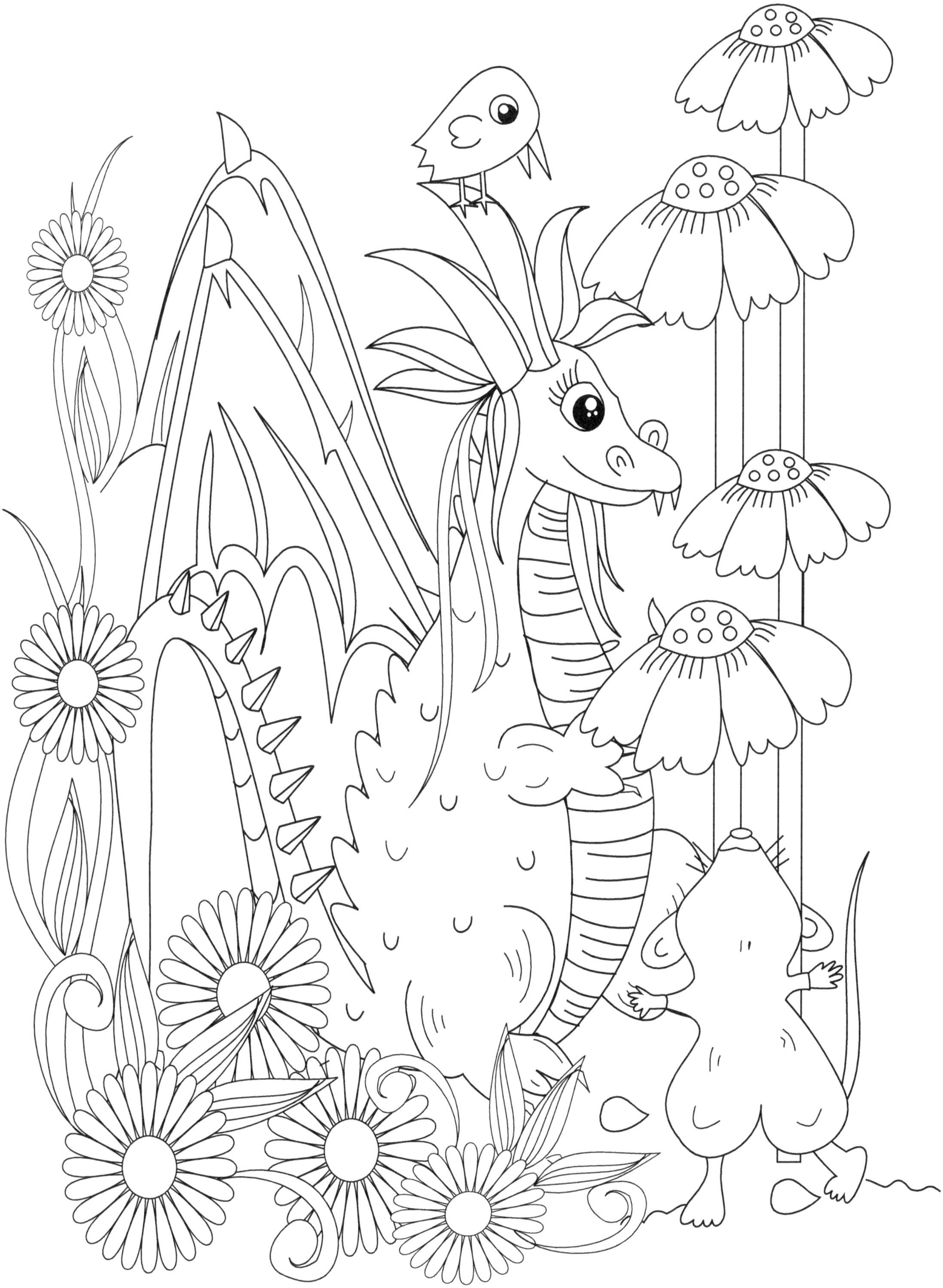

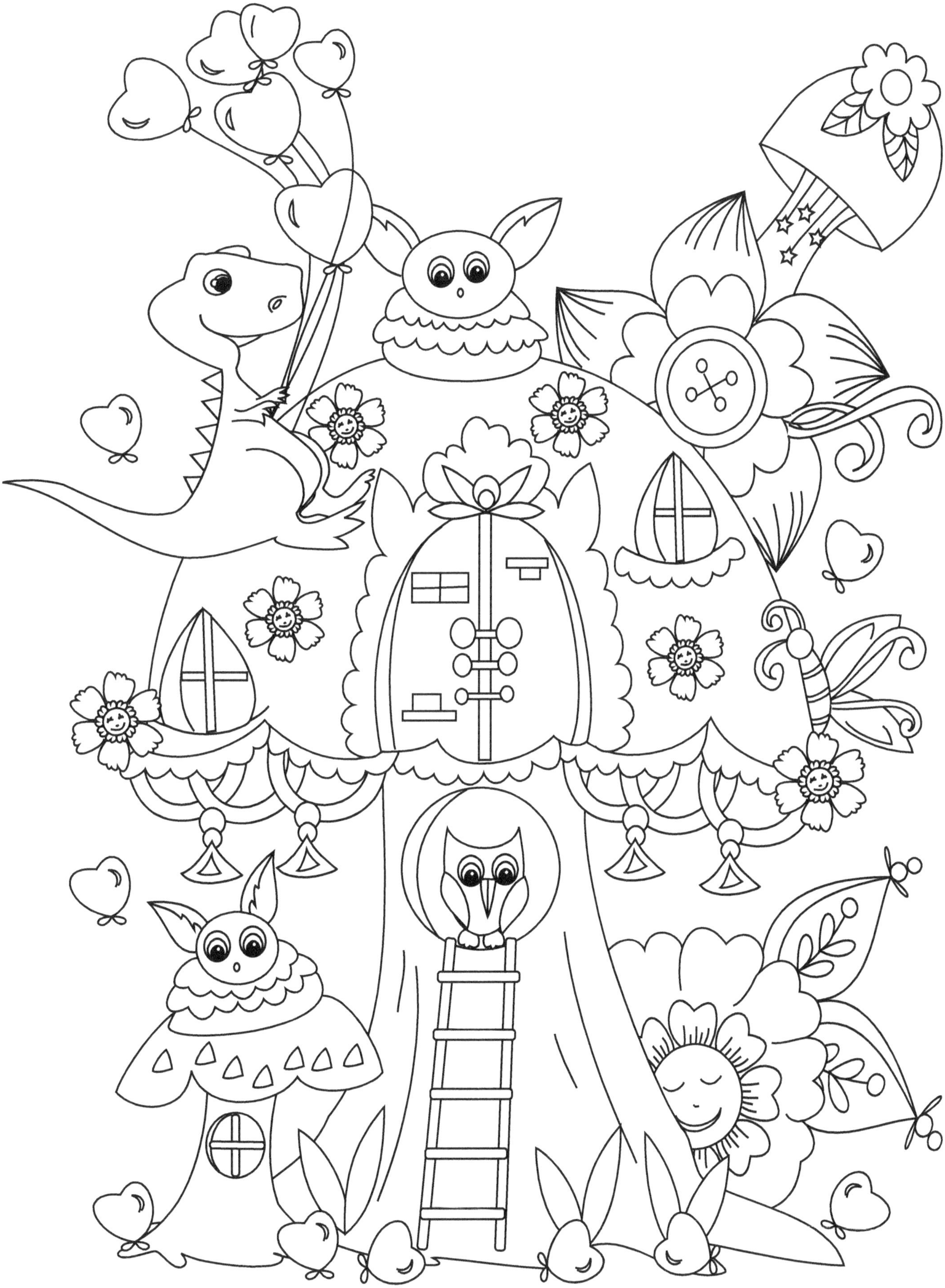

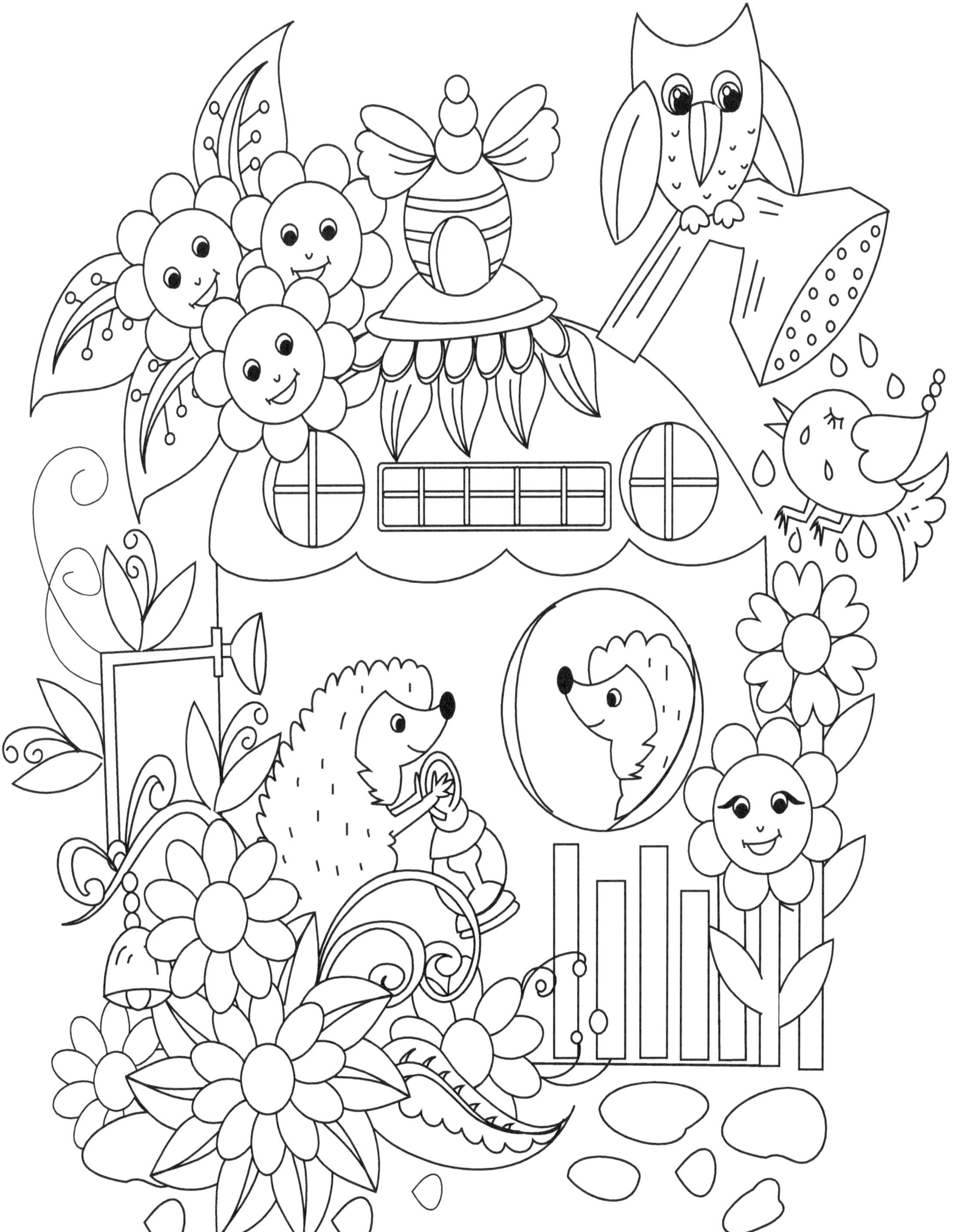

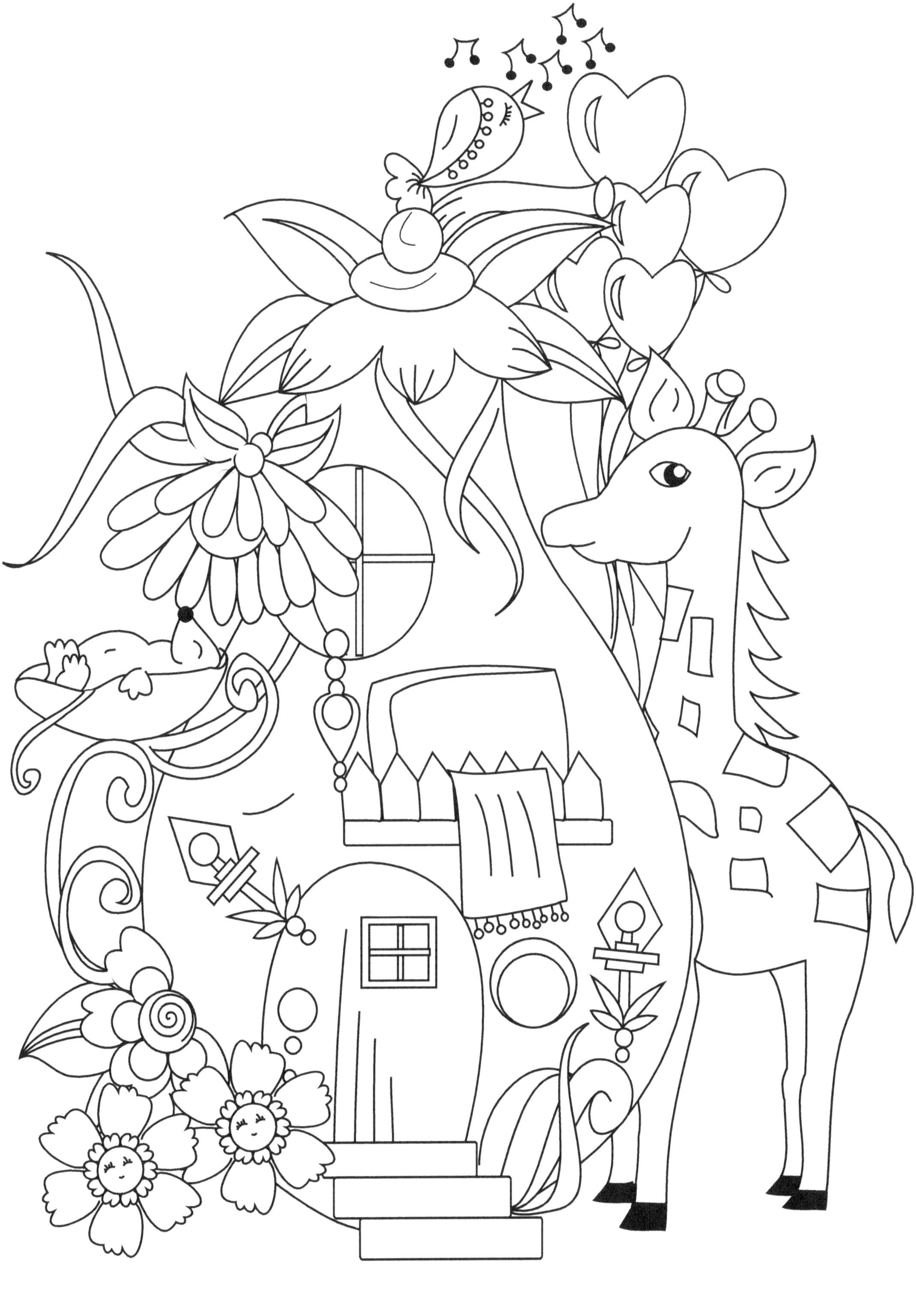

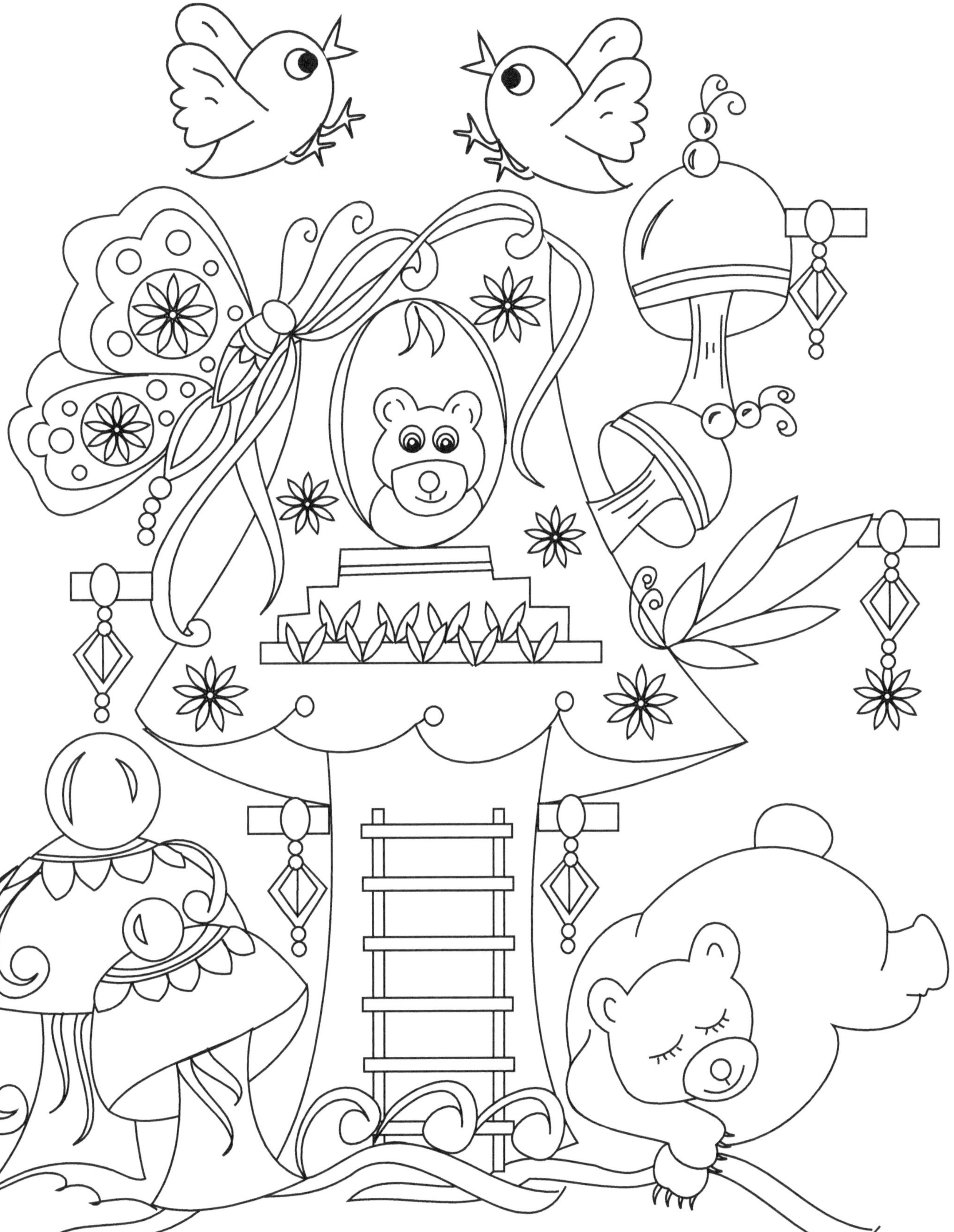

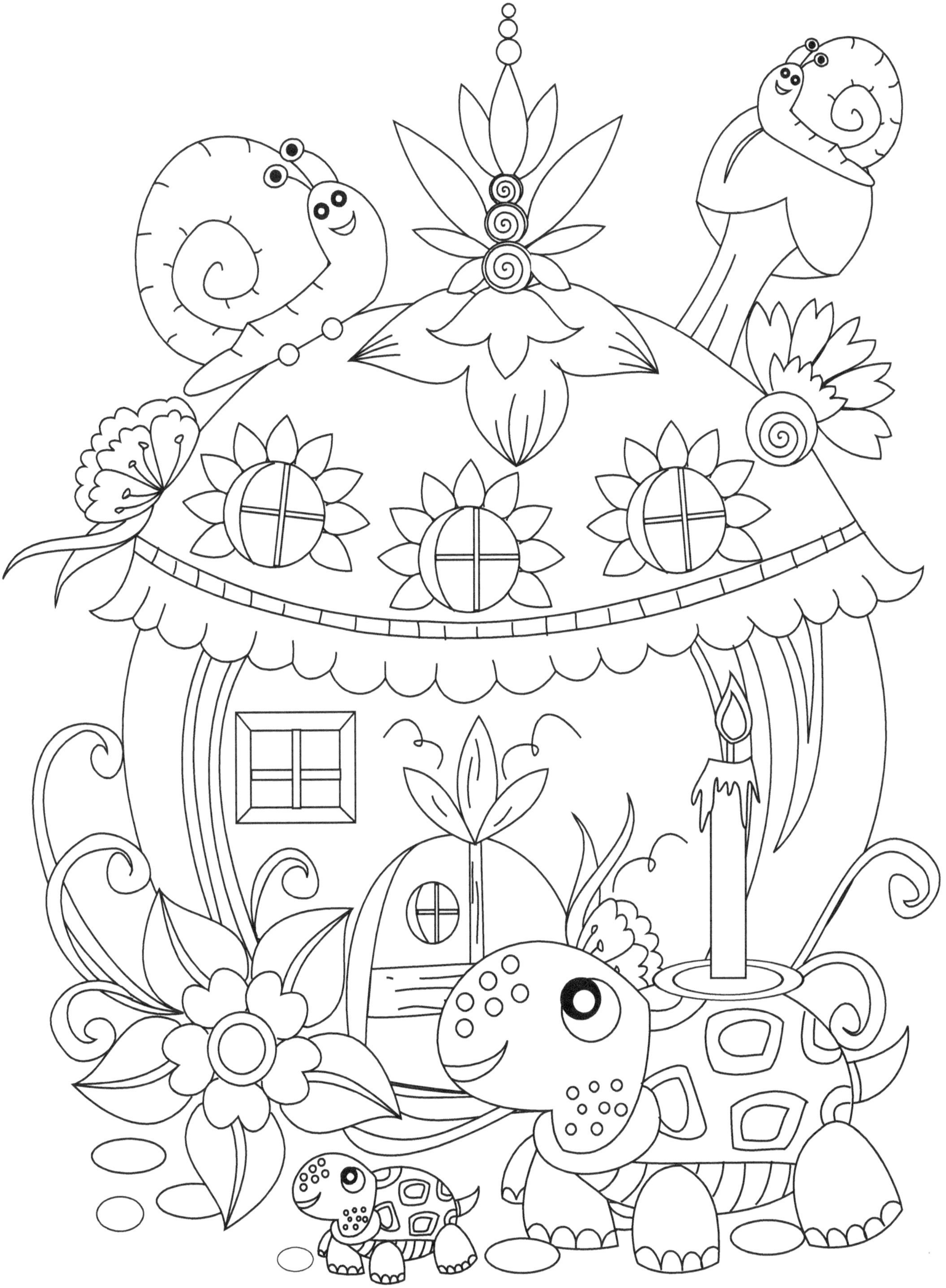

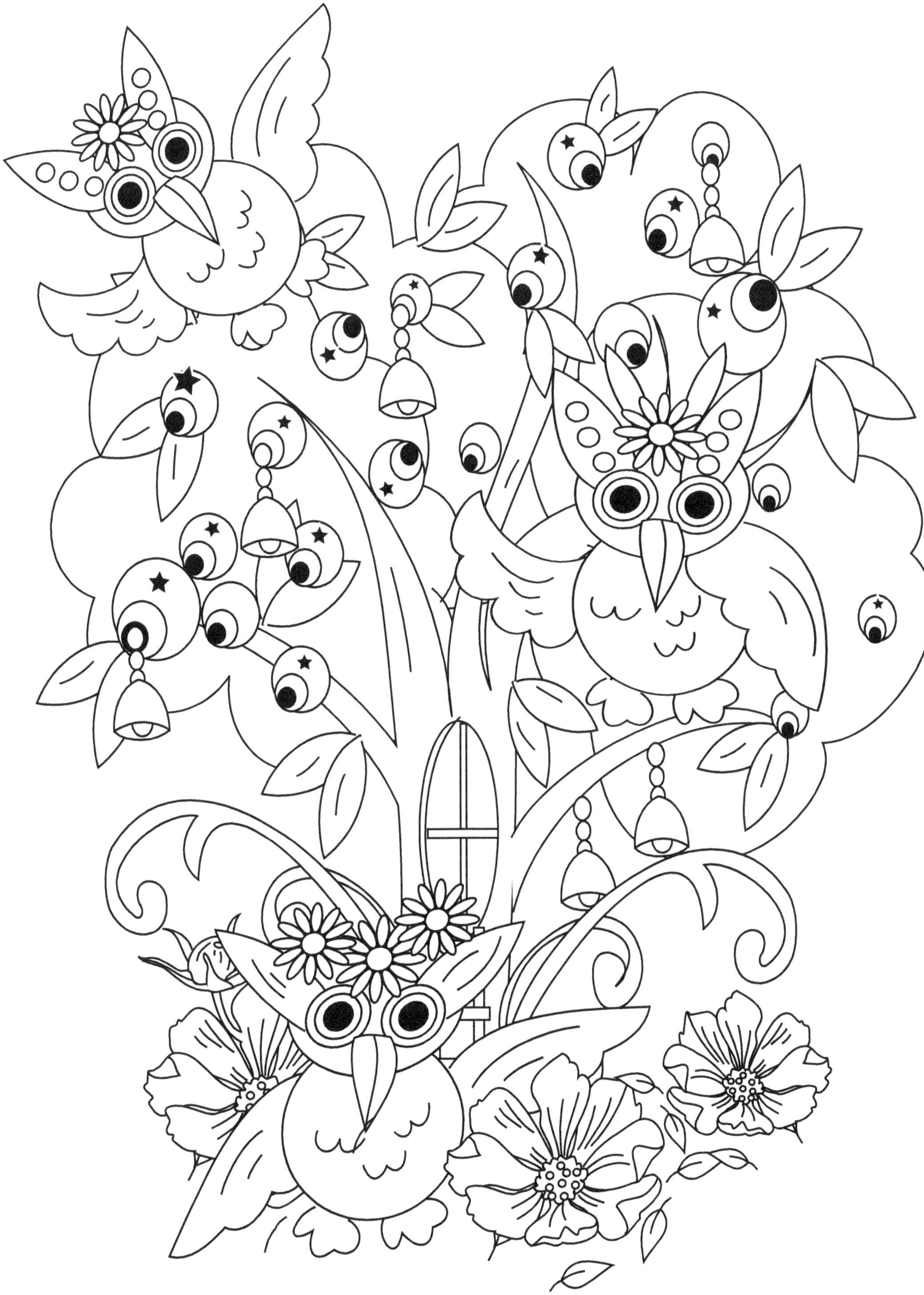

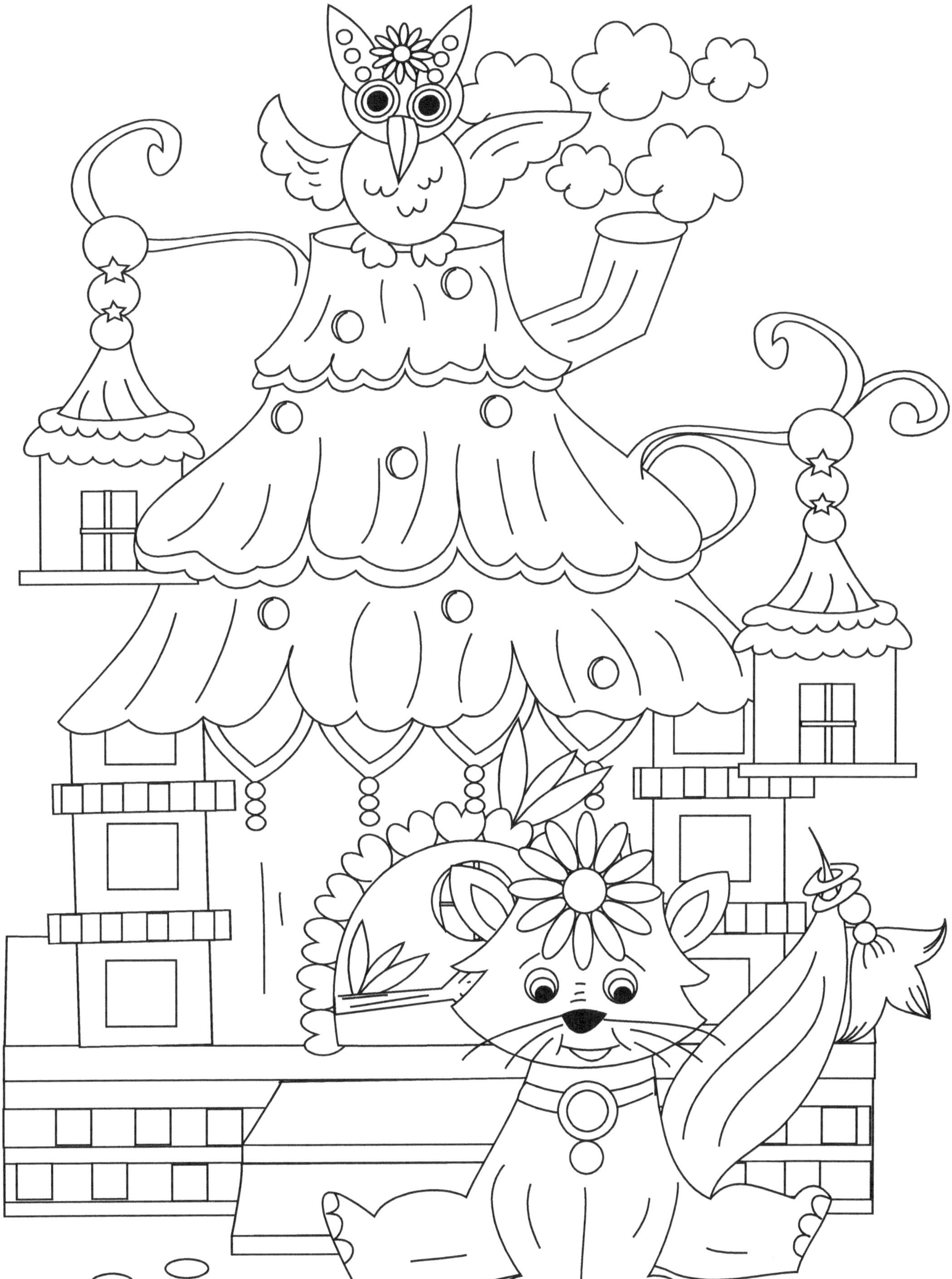

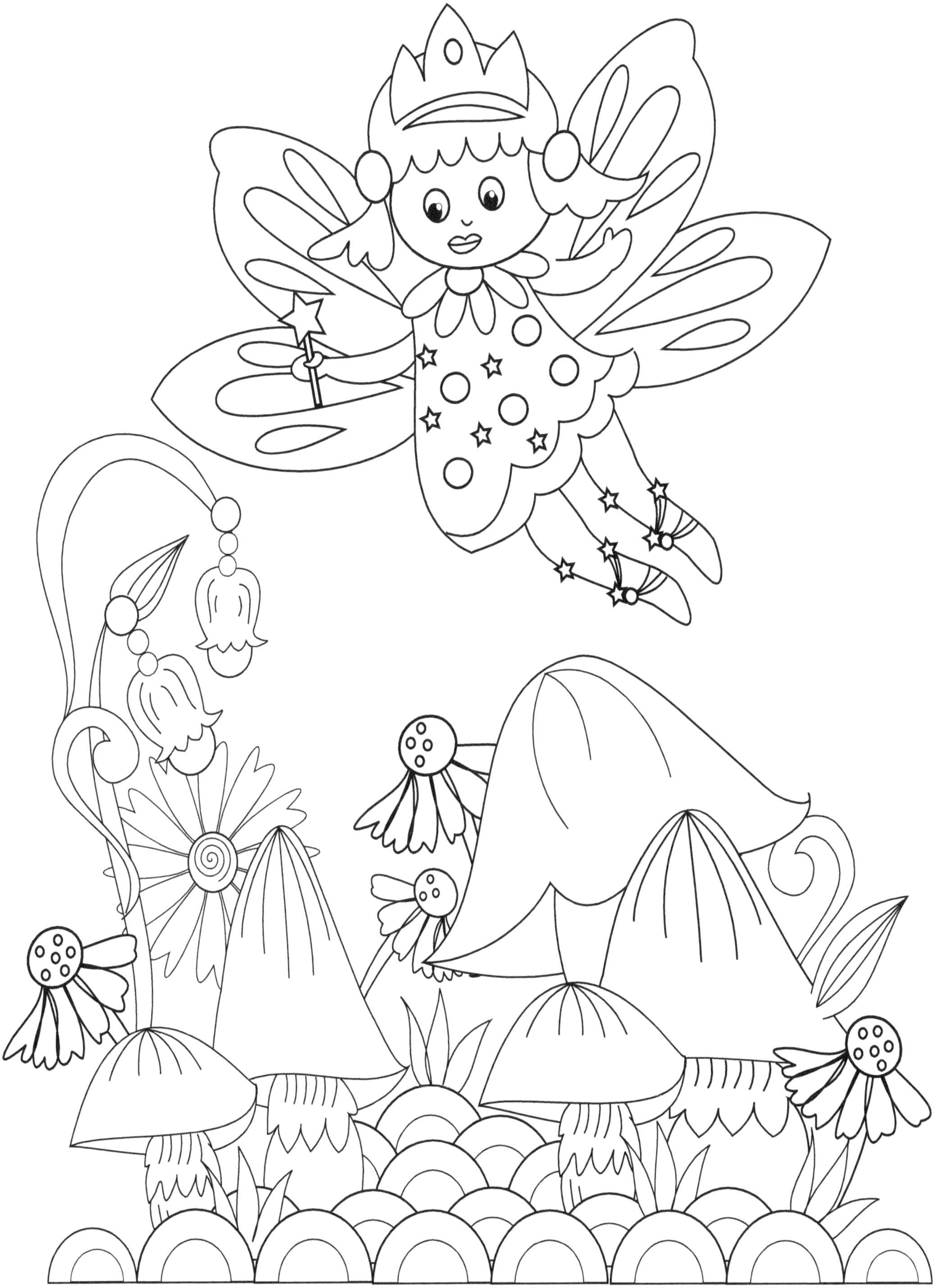

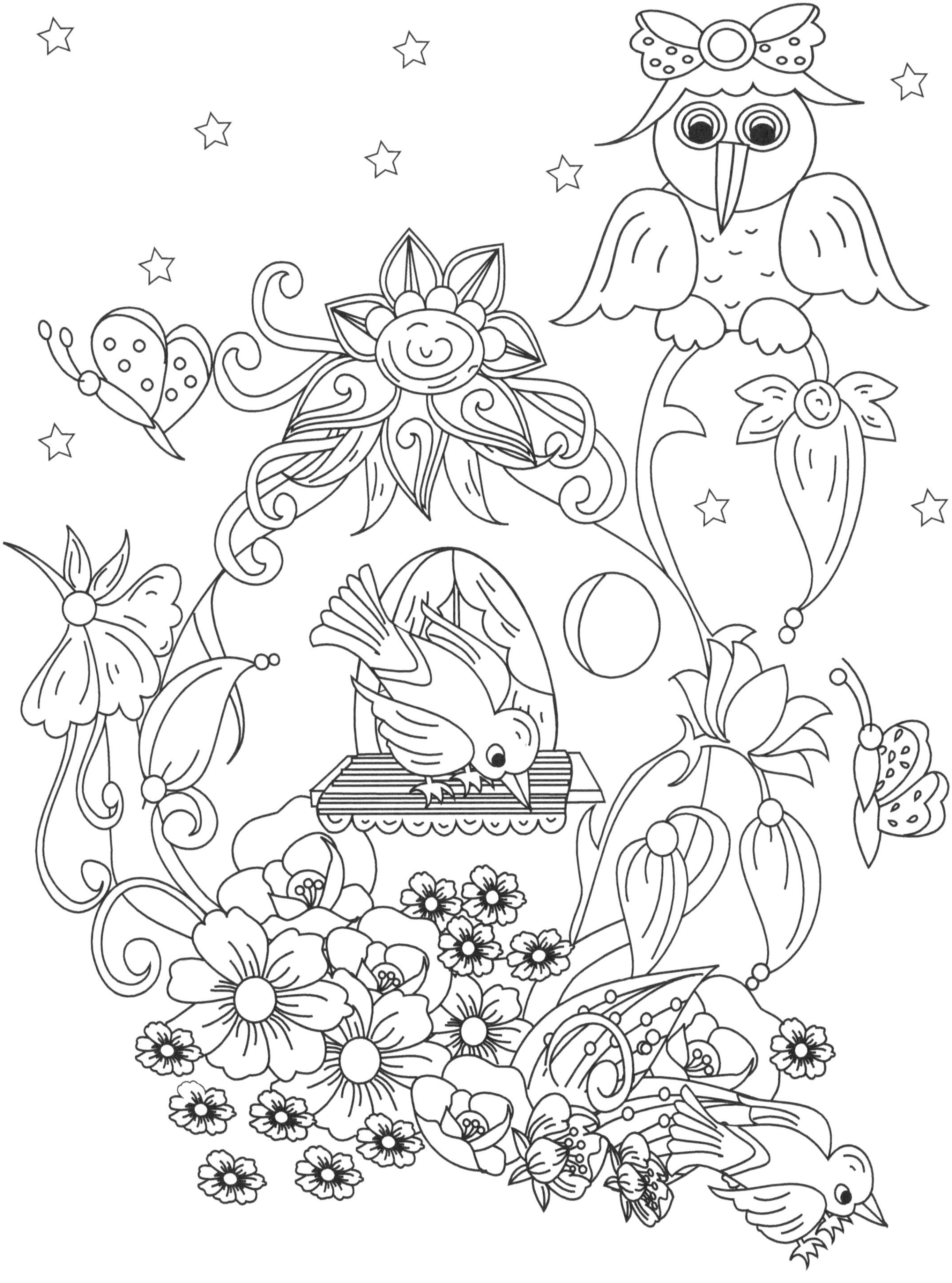

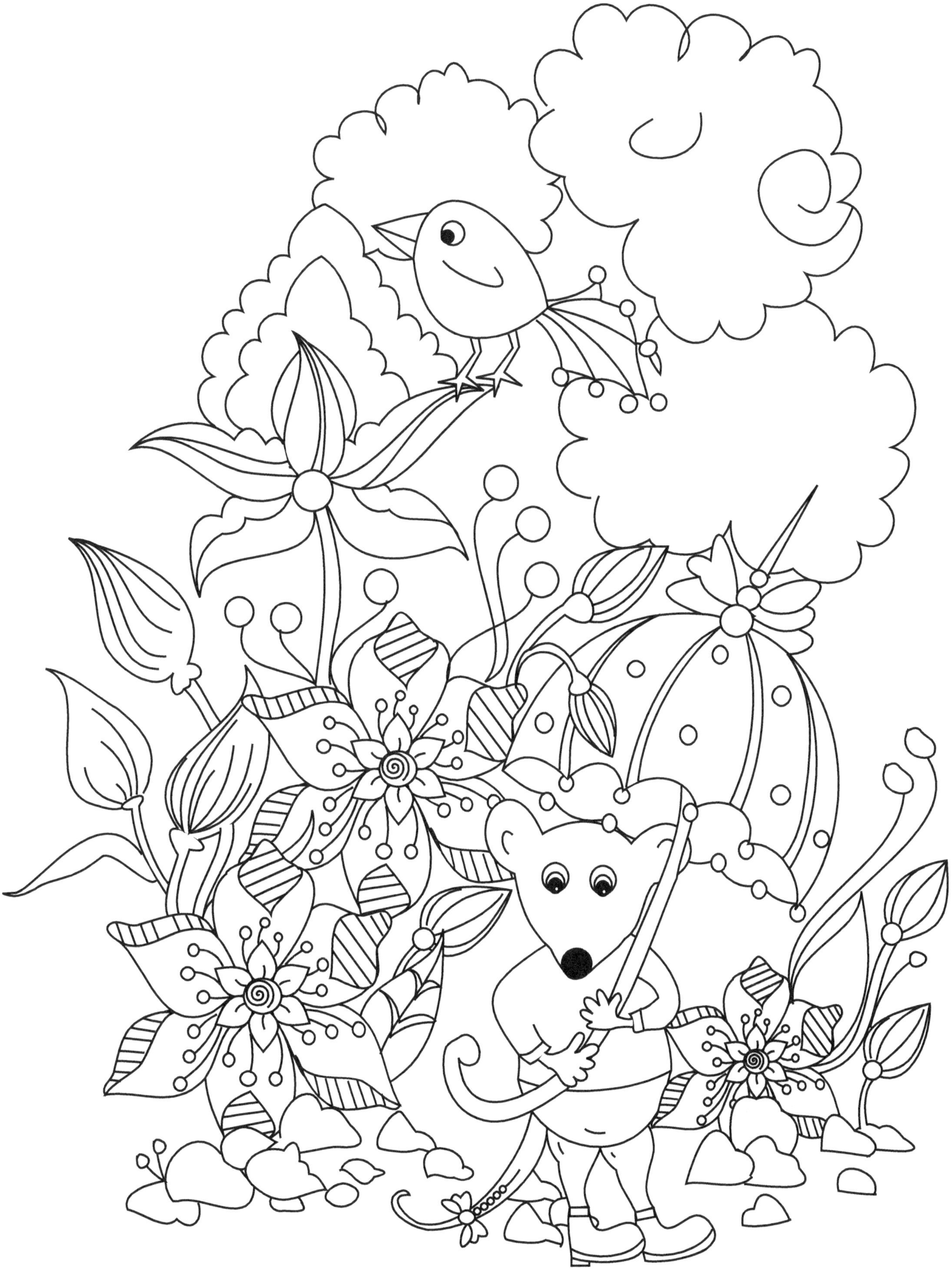

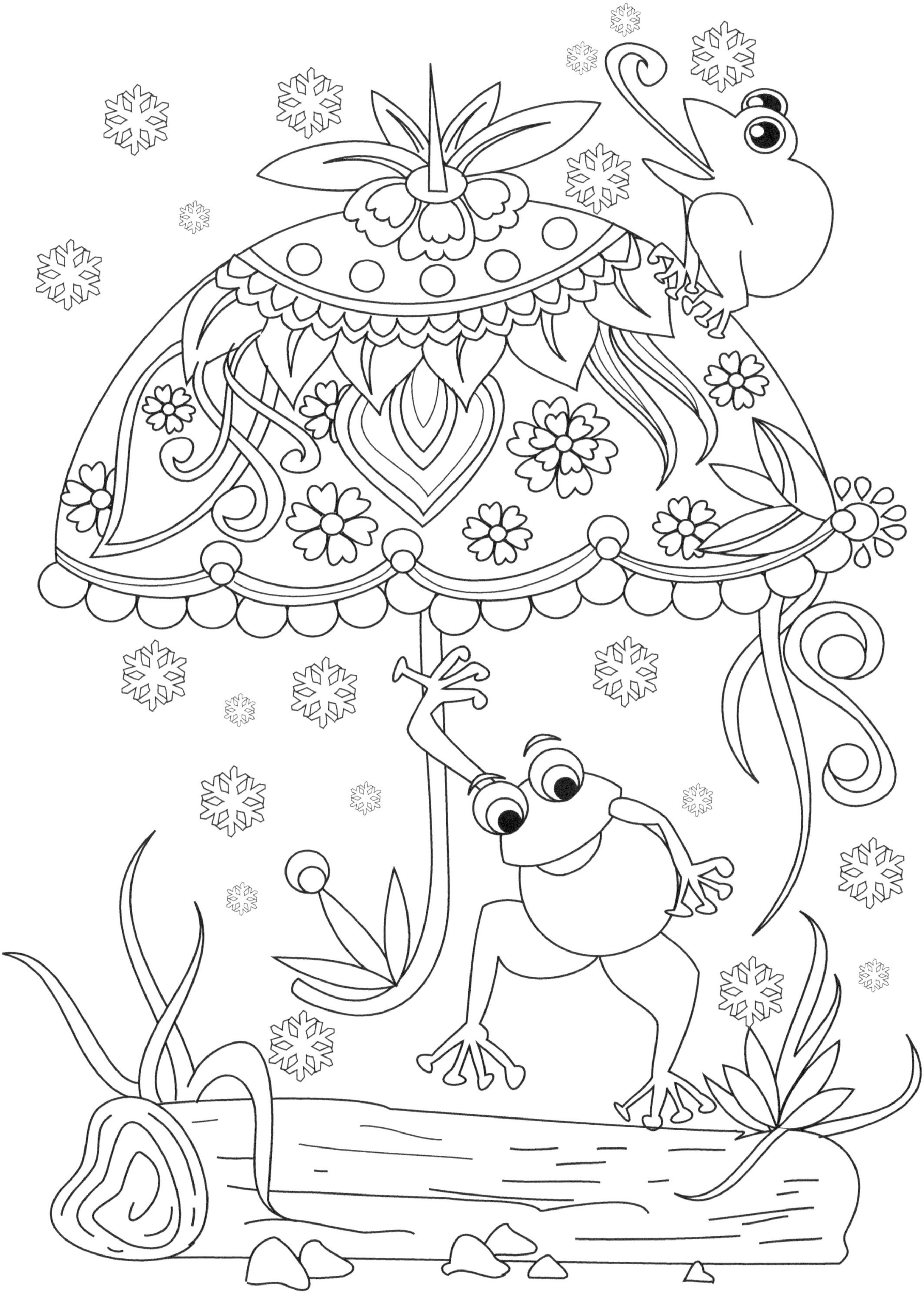

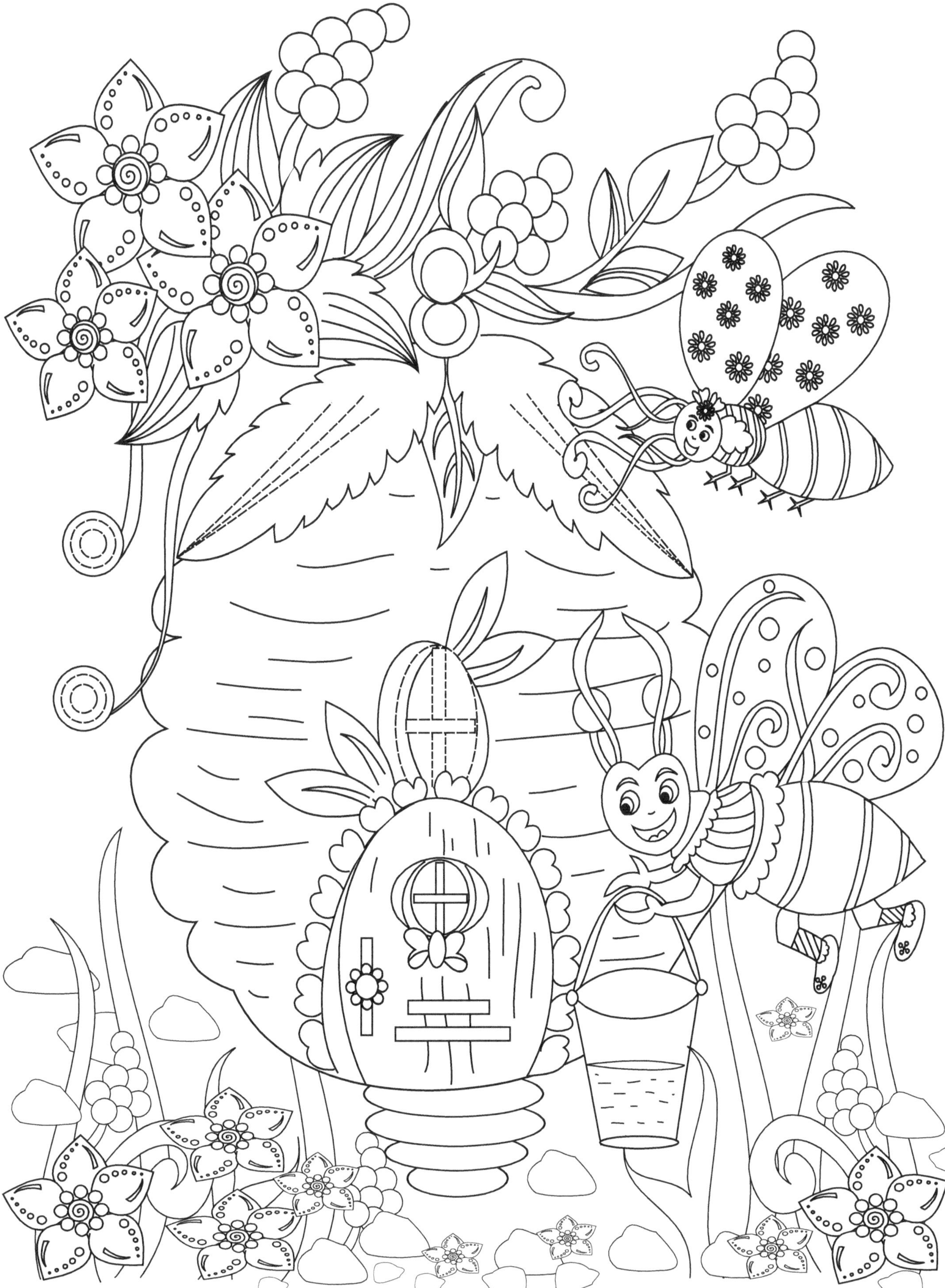

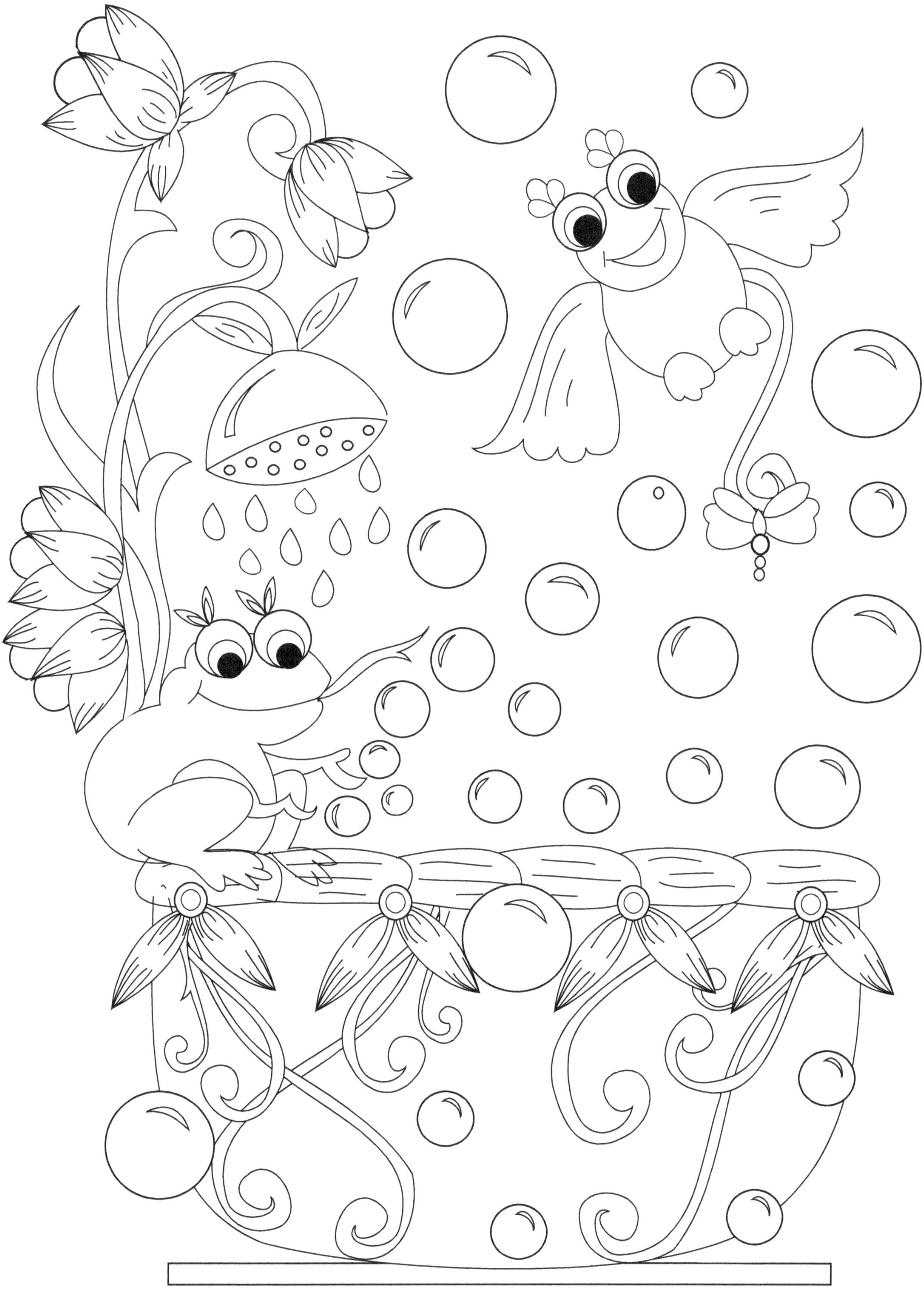

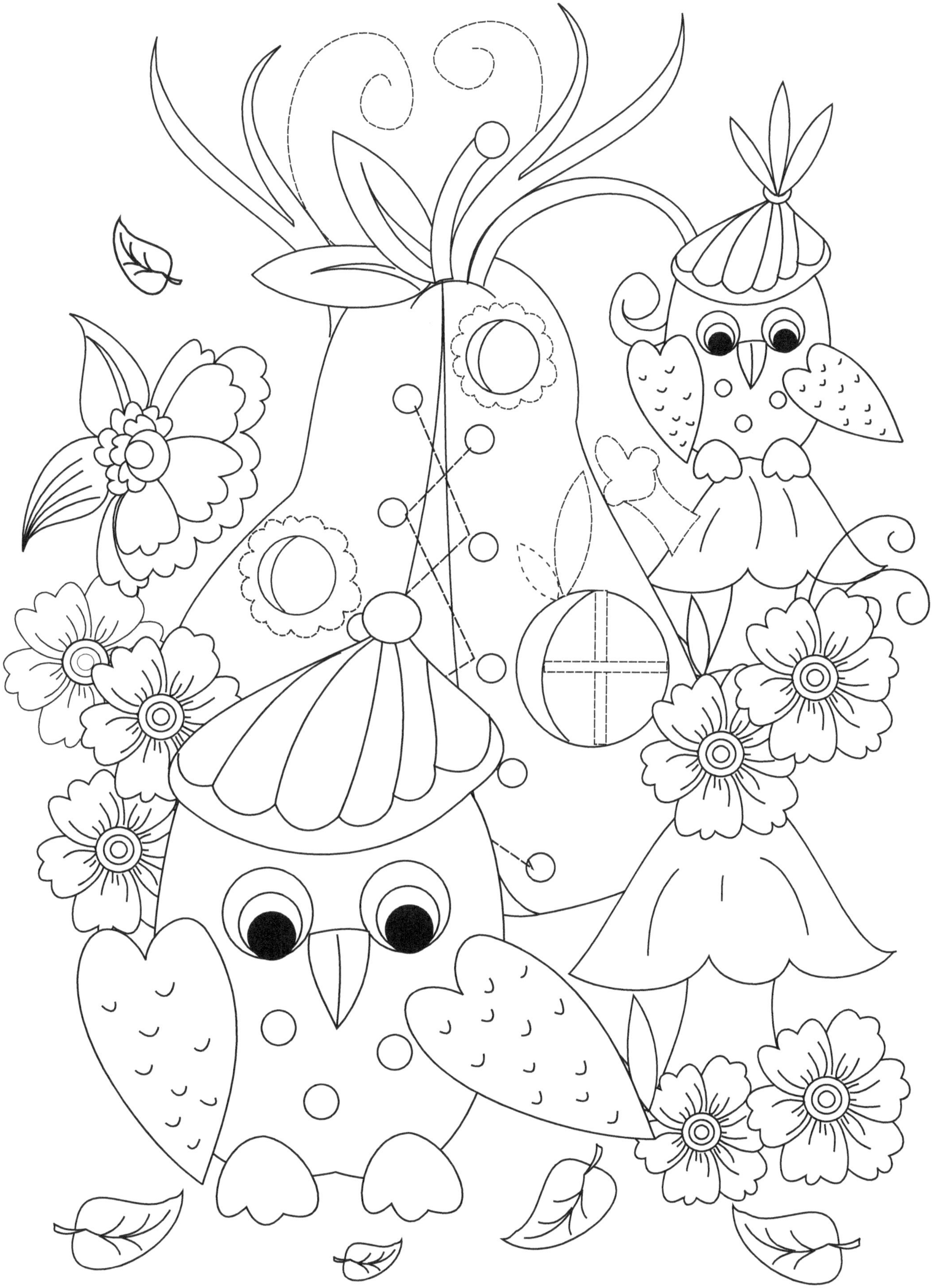

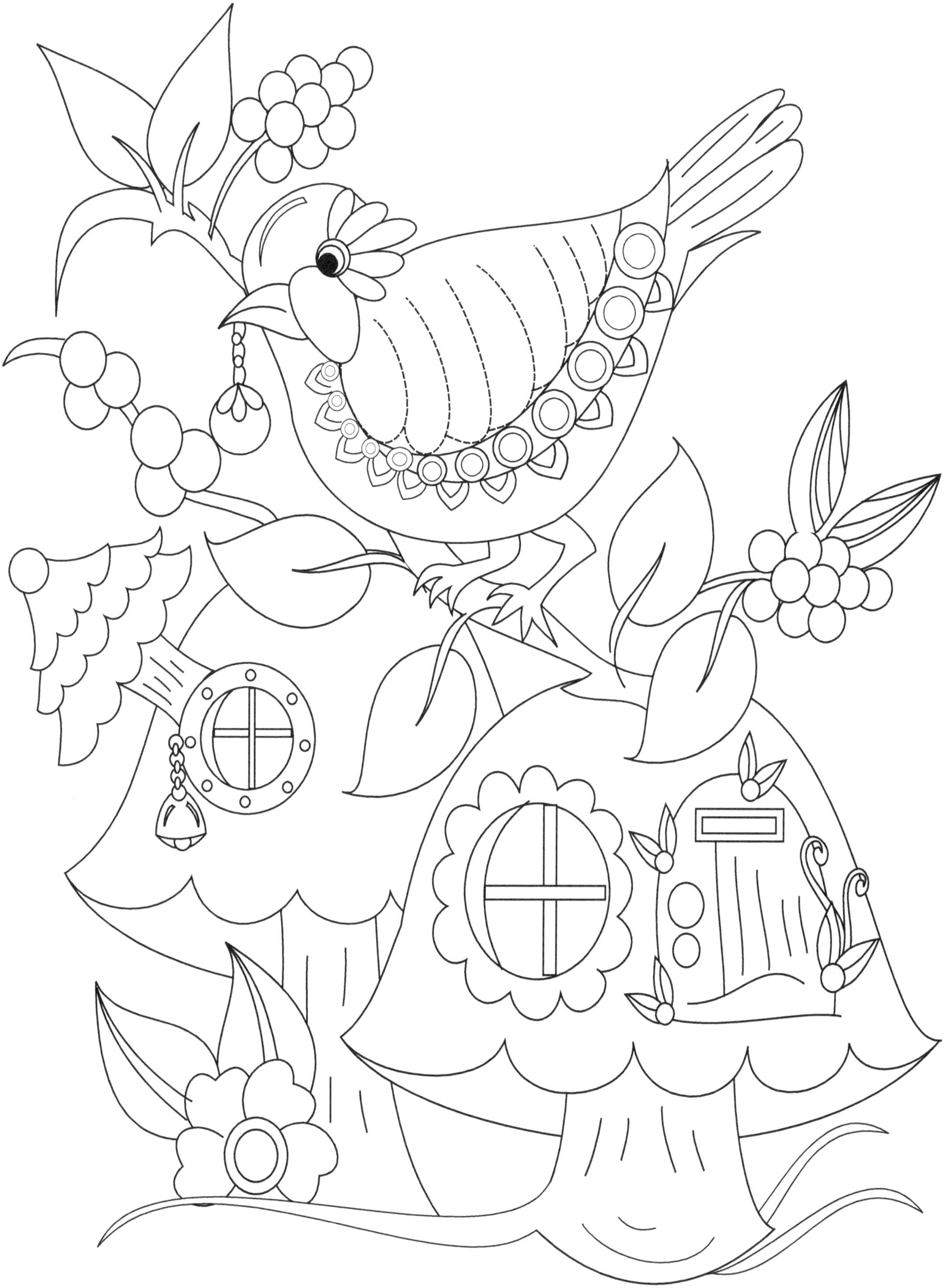

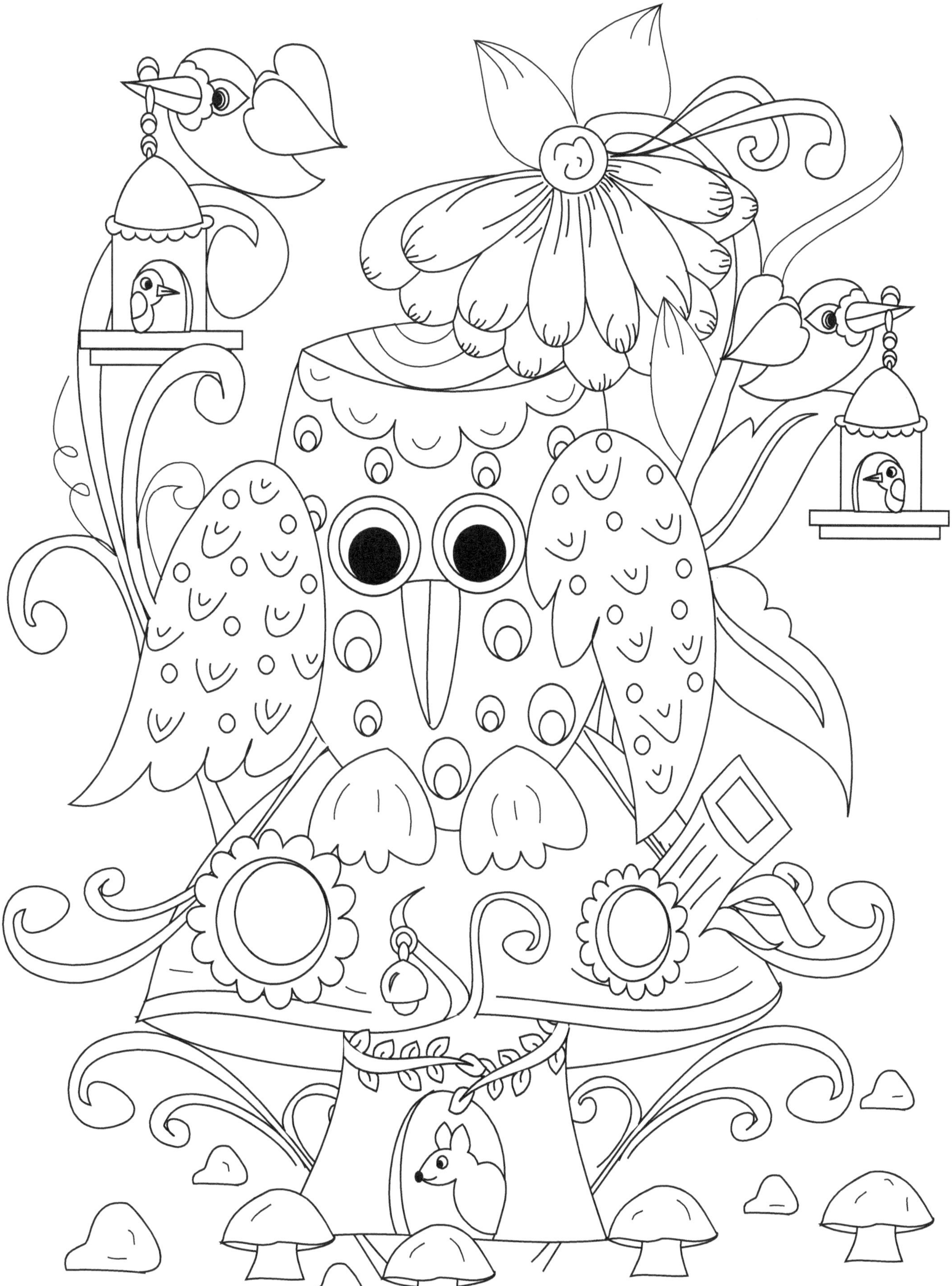

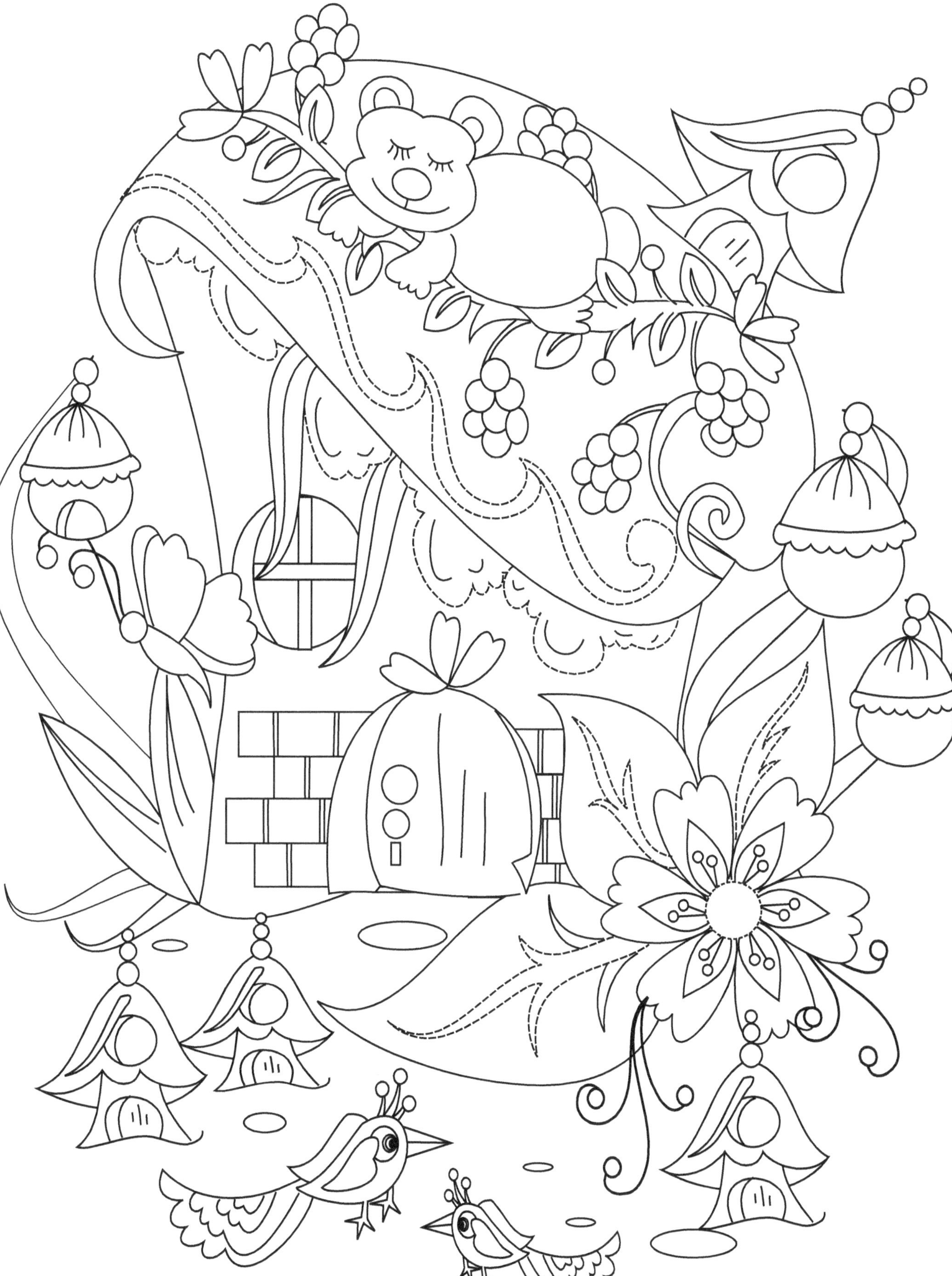

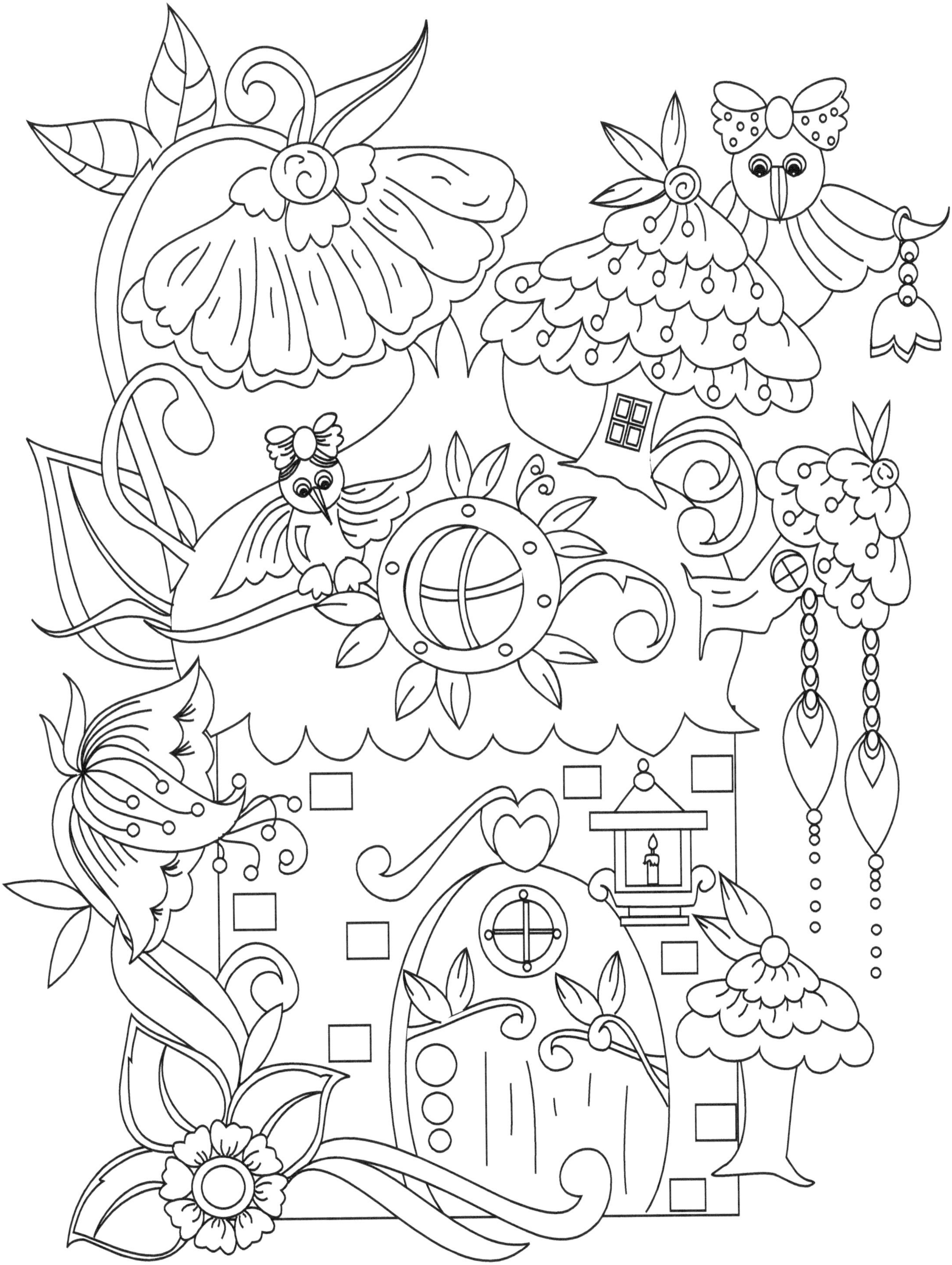

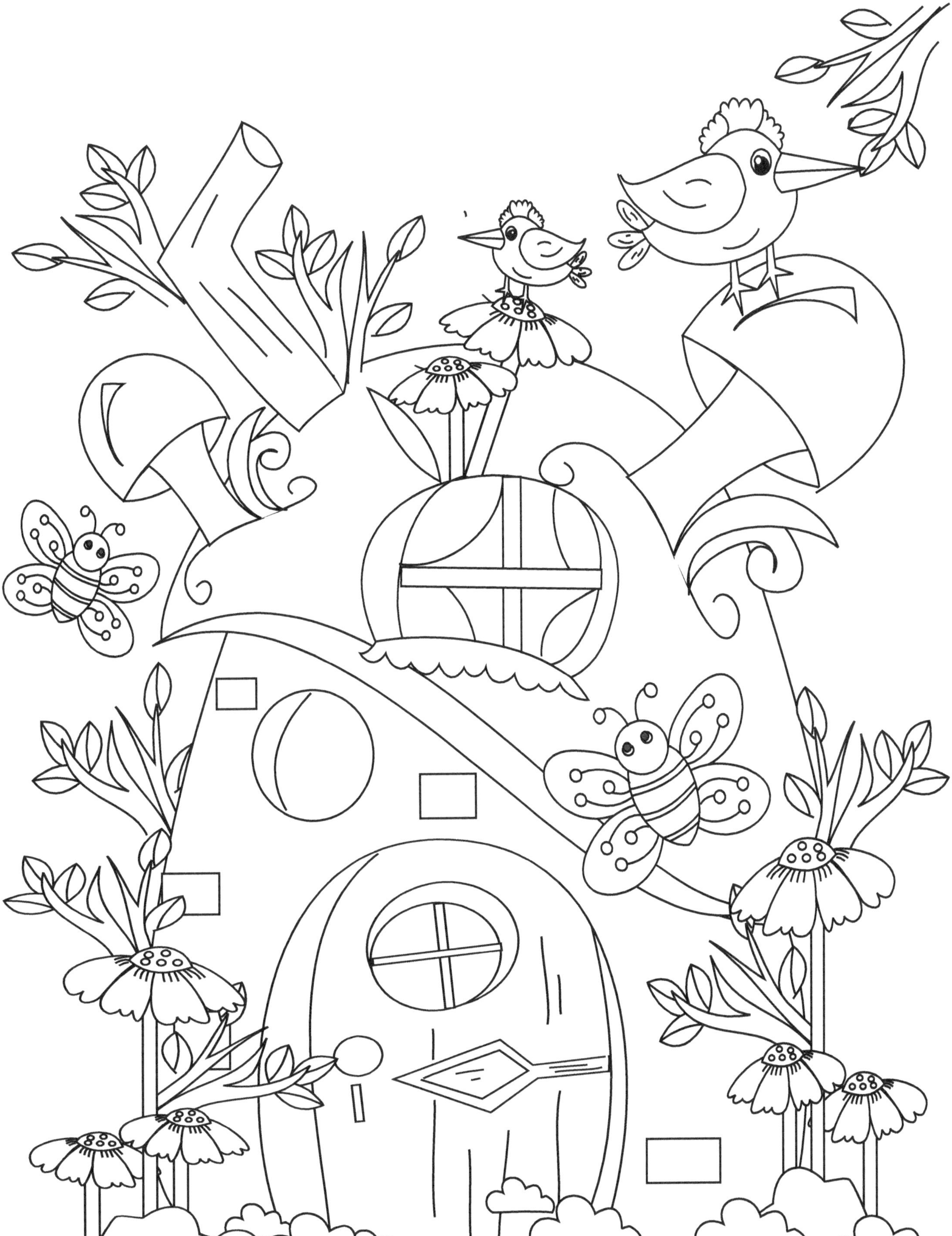

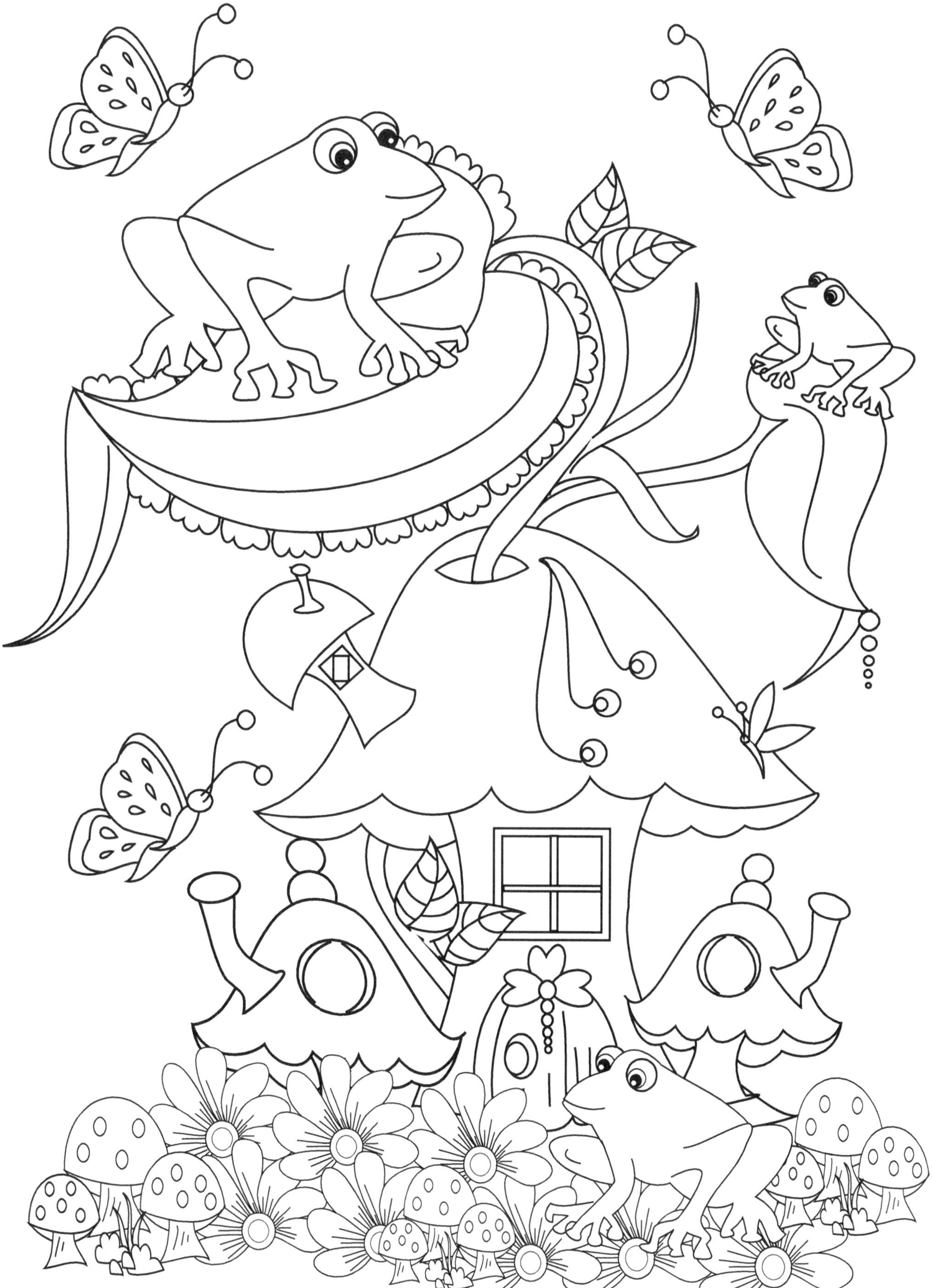

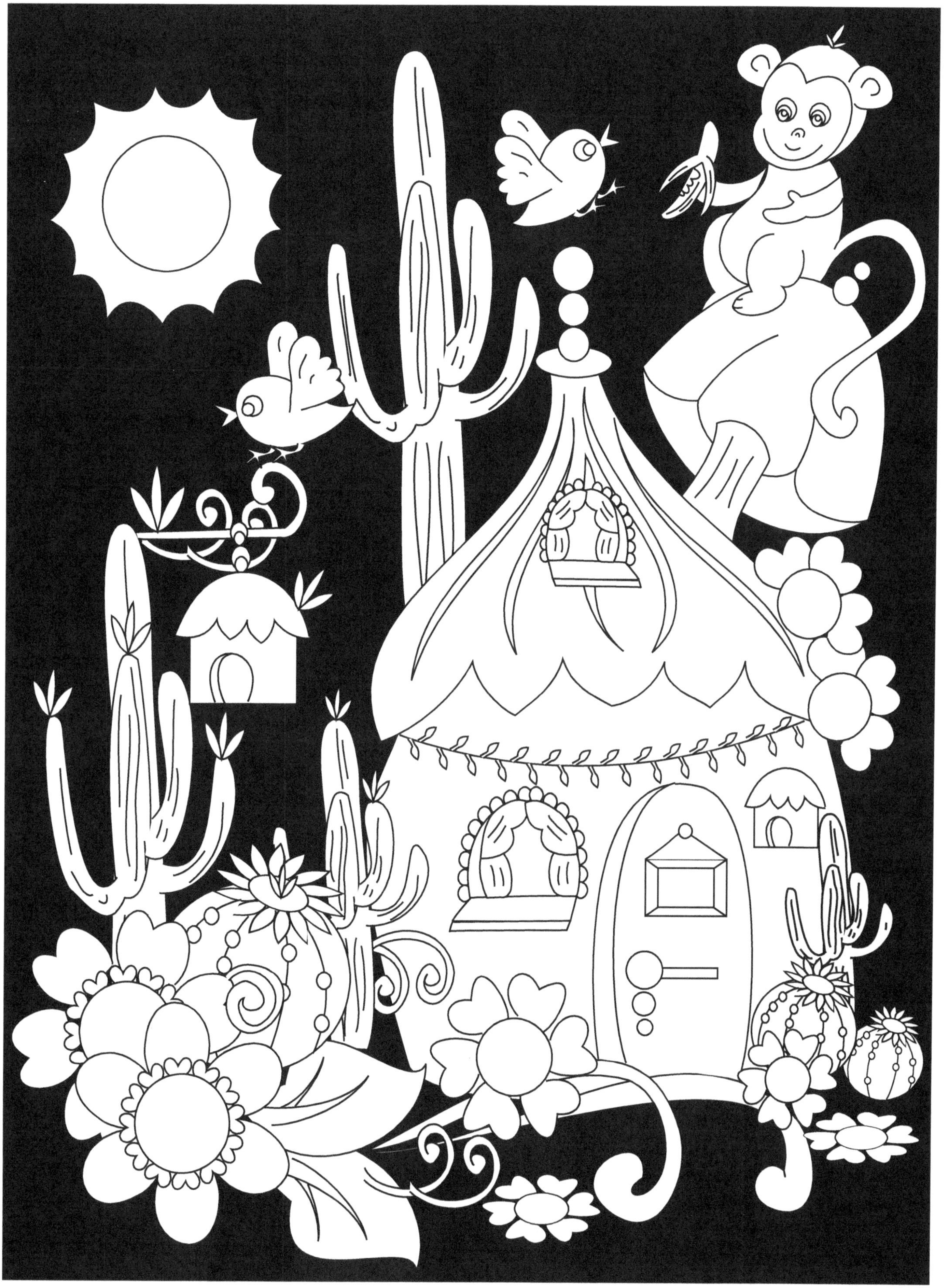

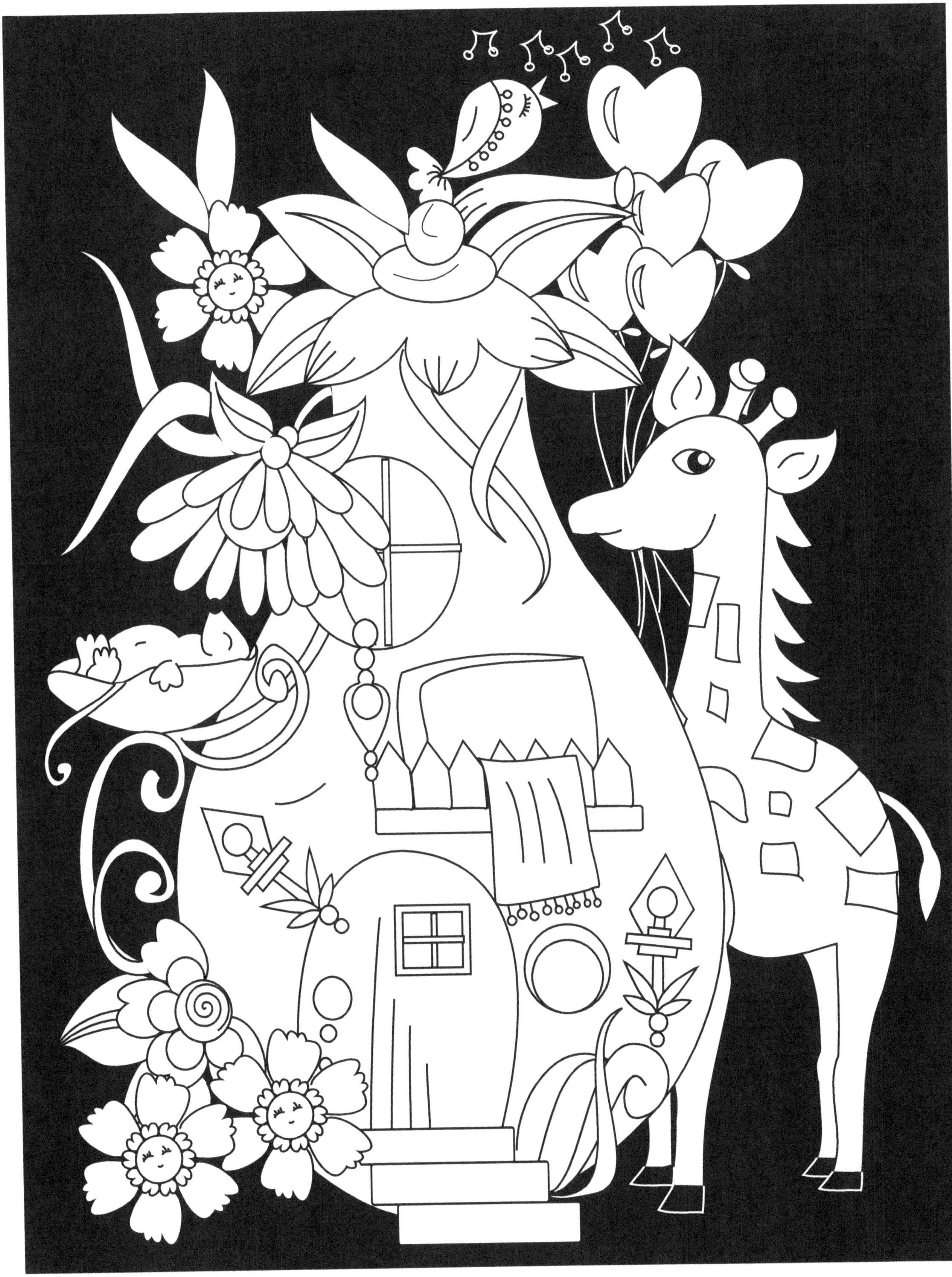

Color test

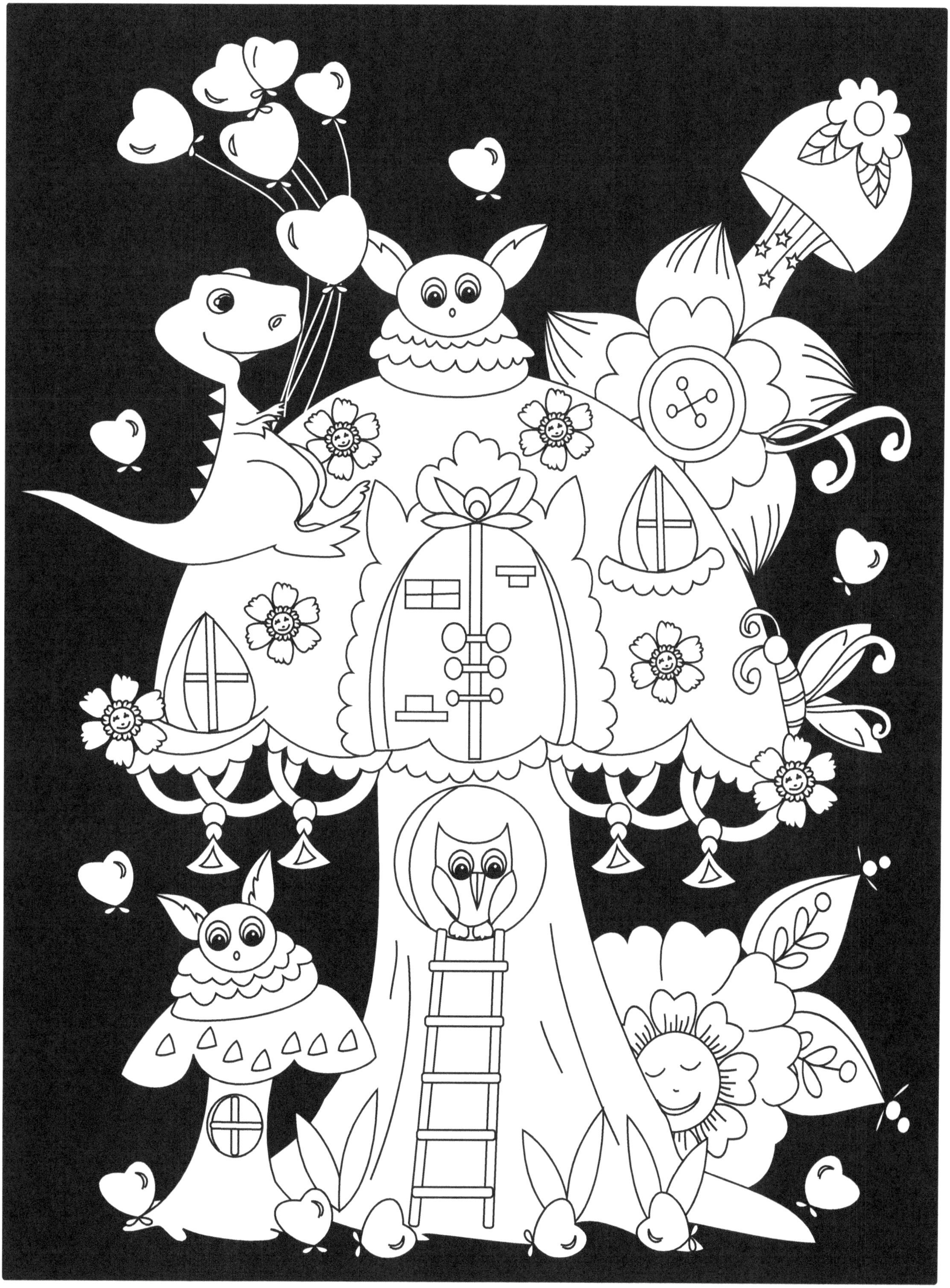

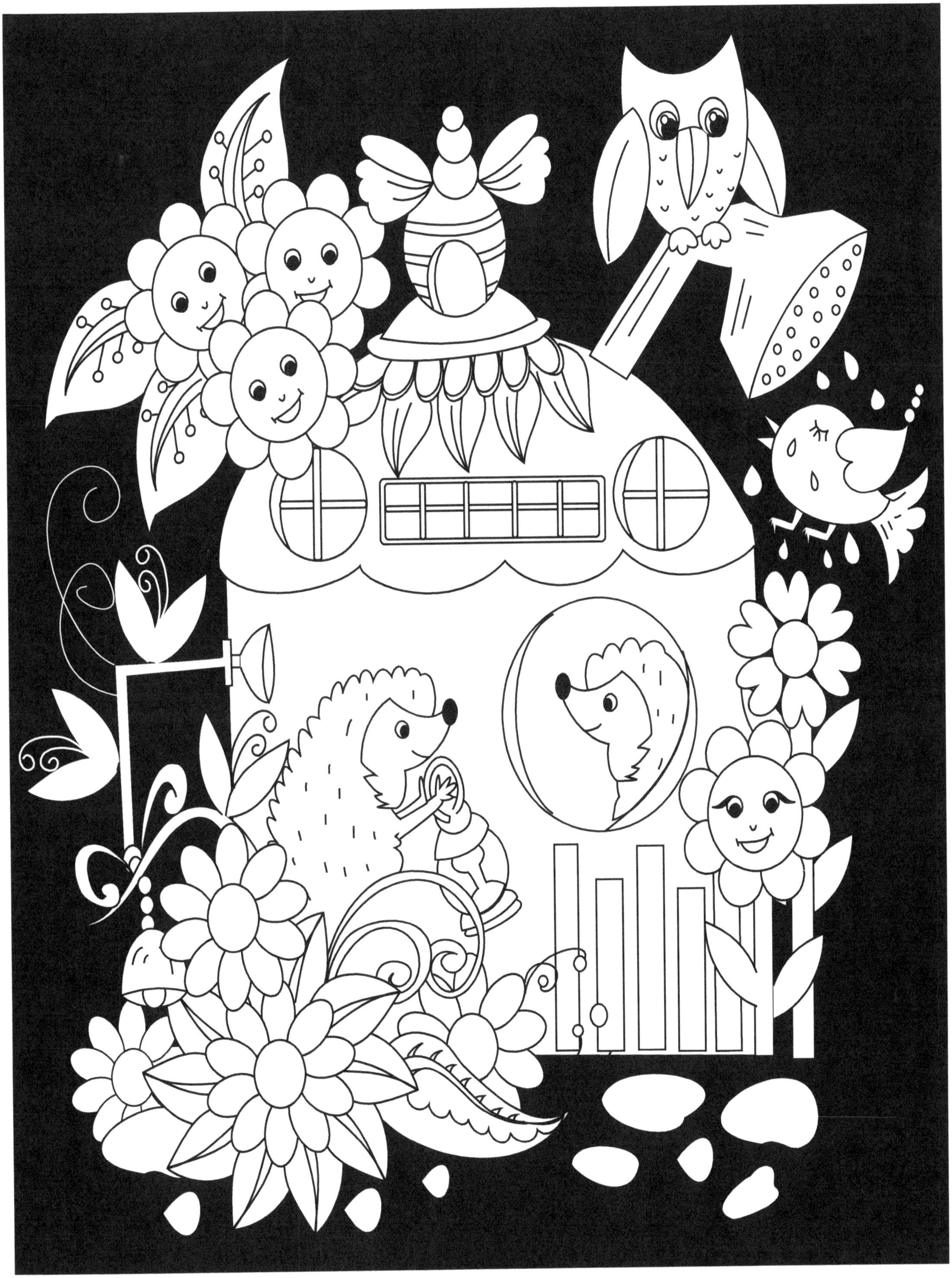

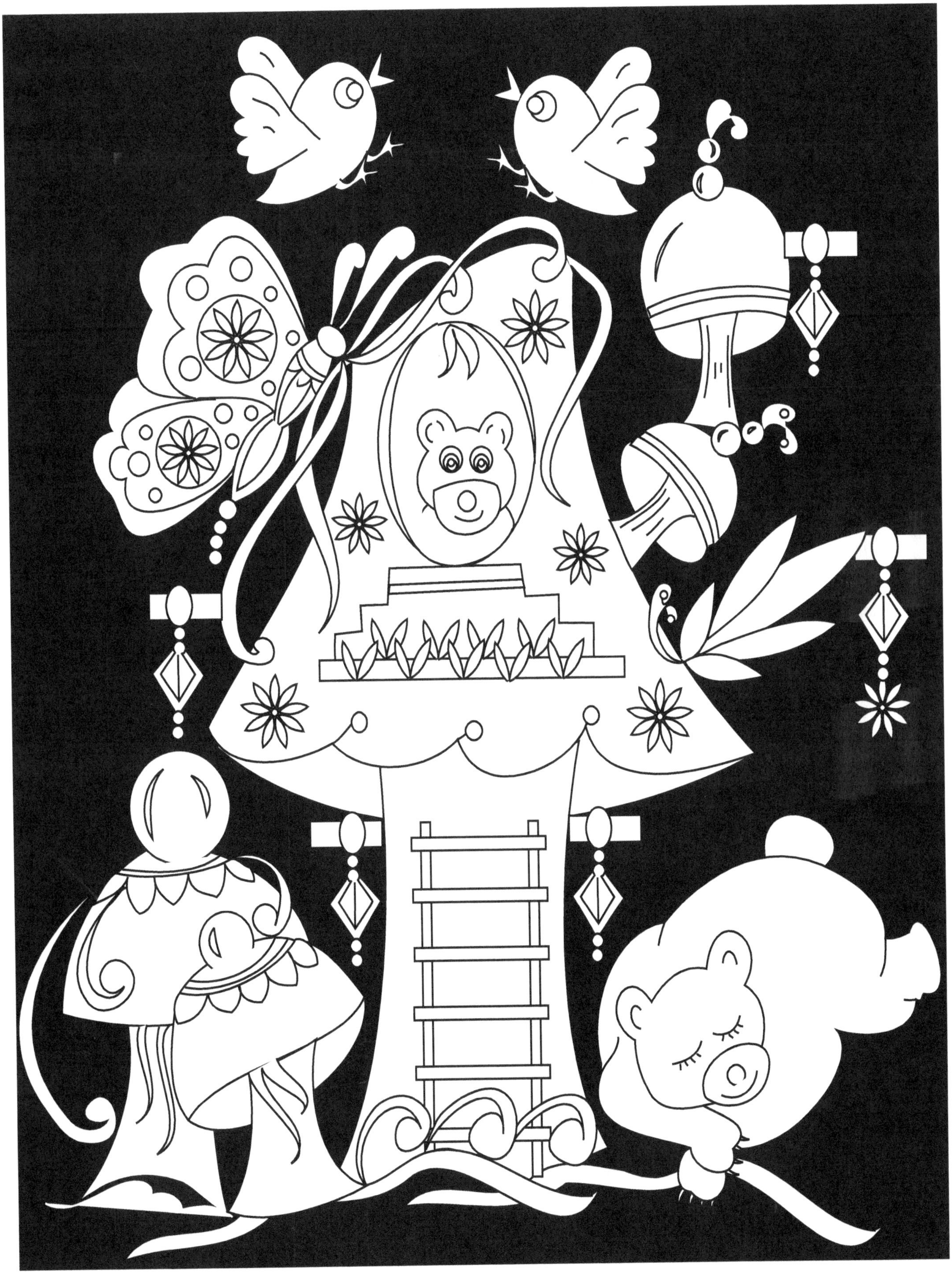

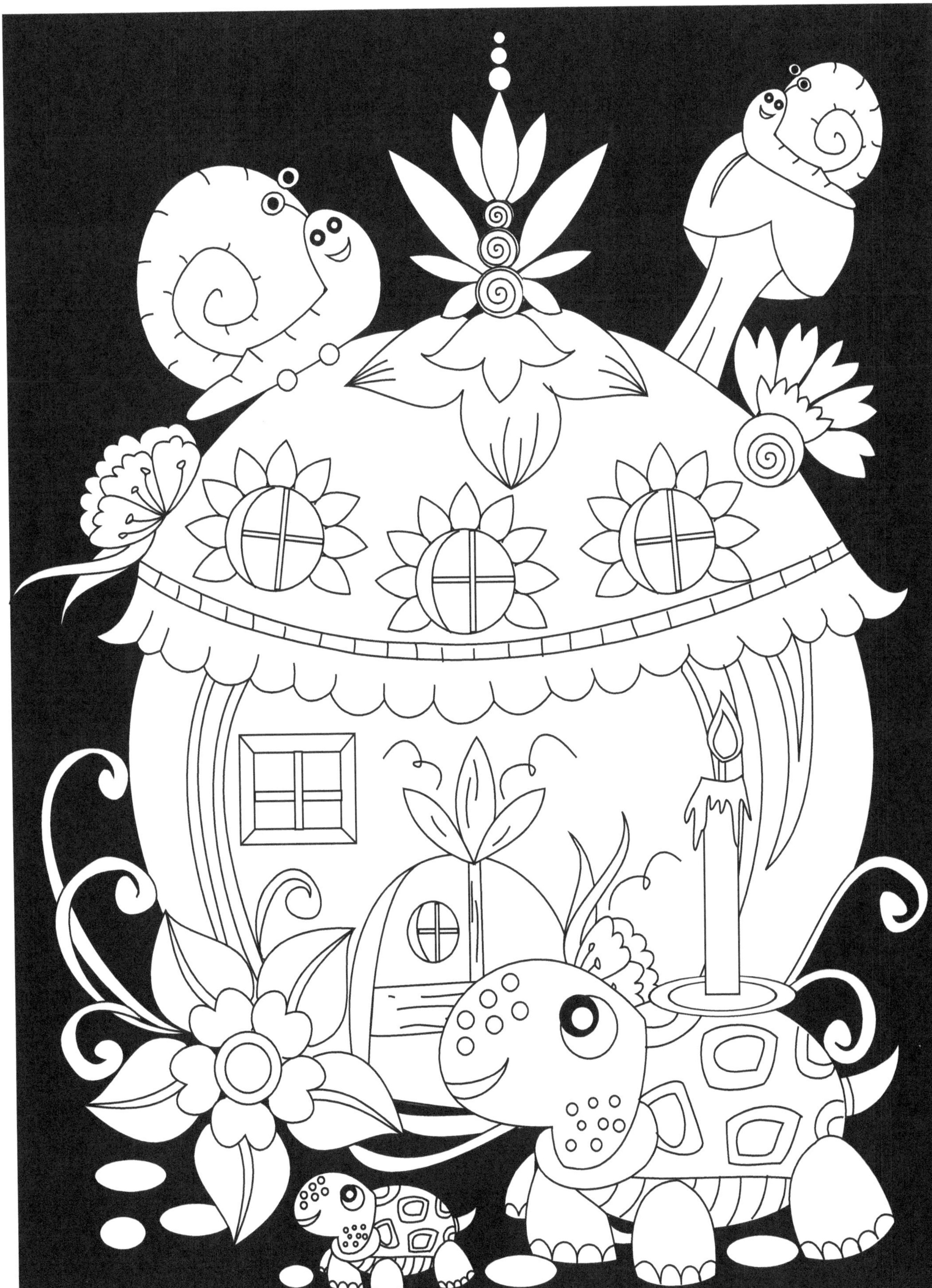

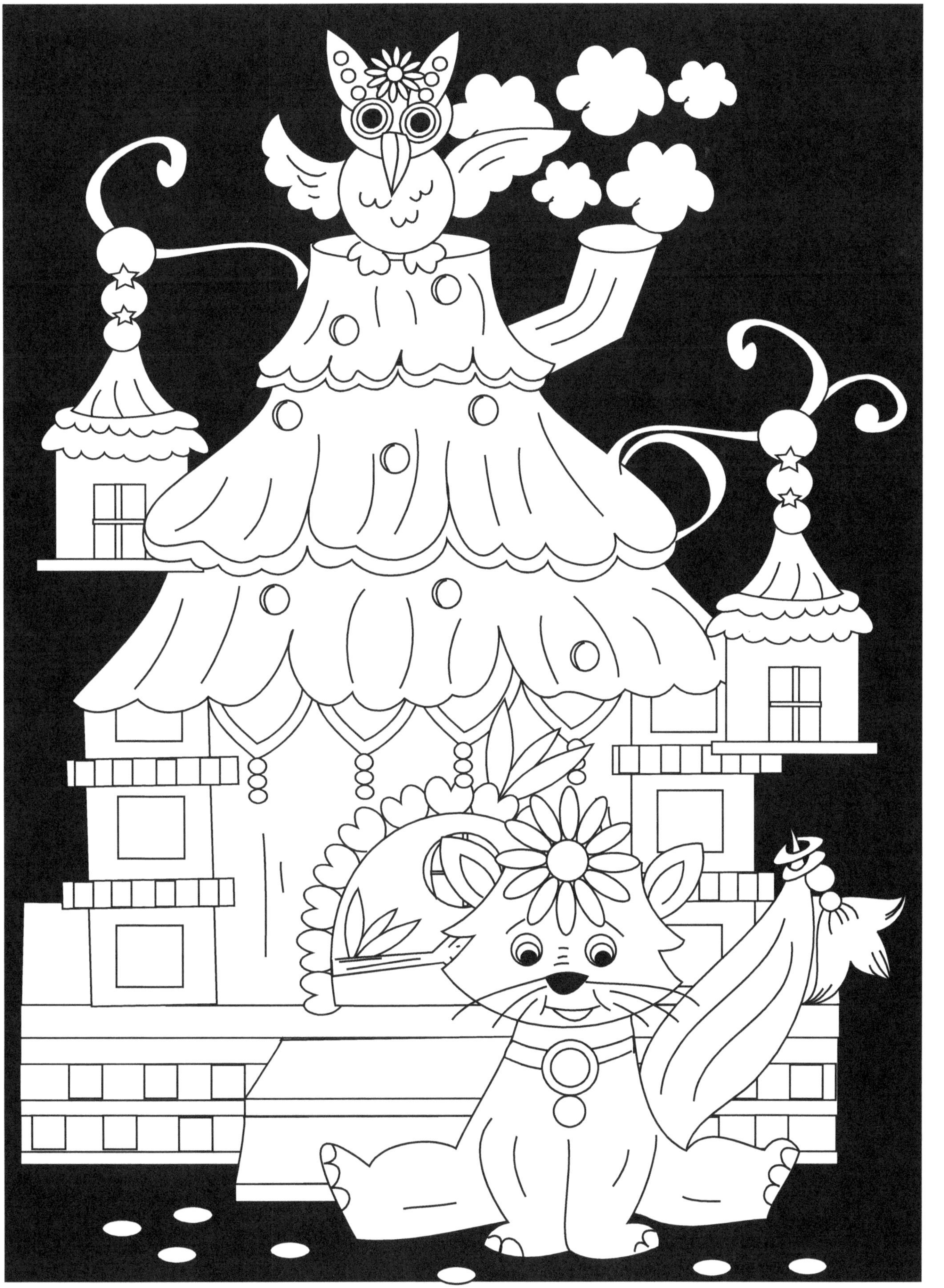

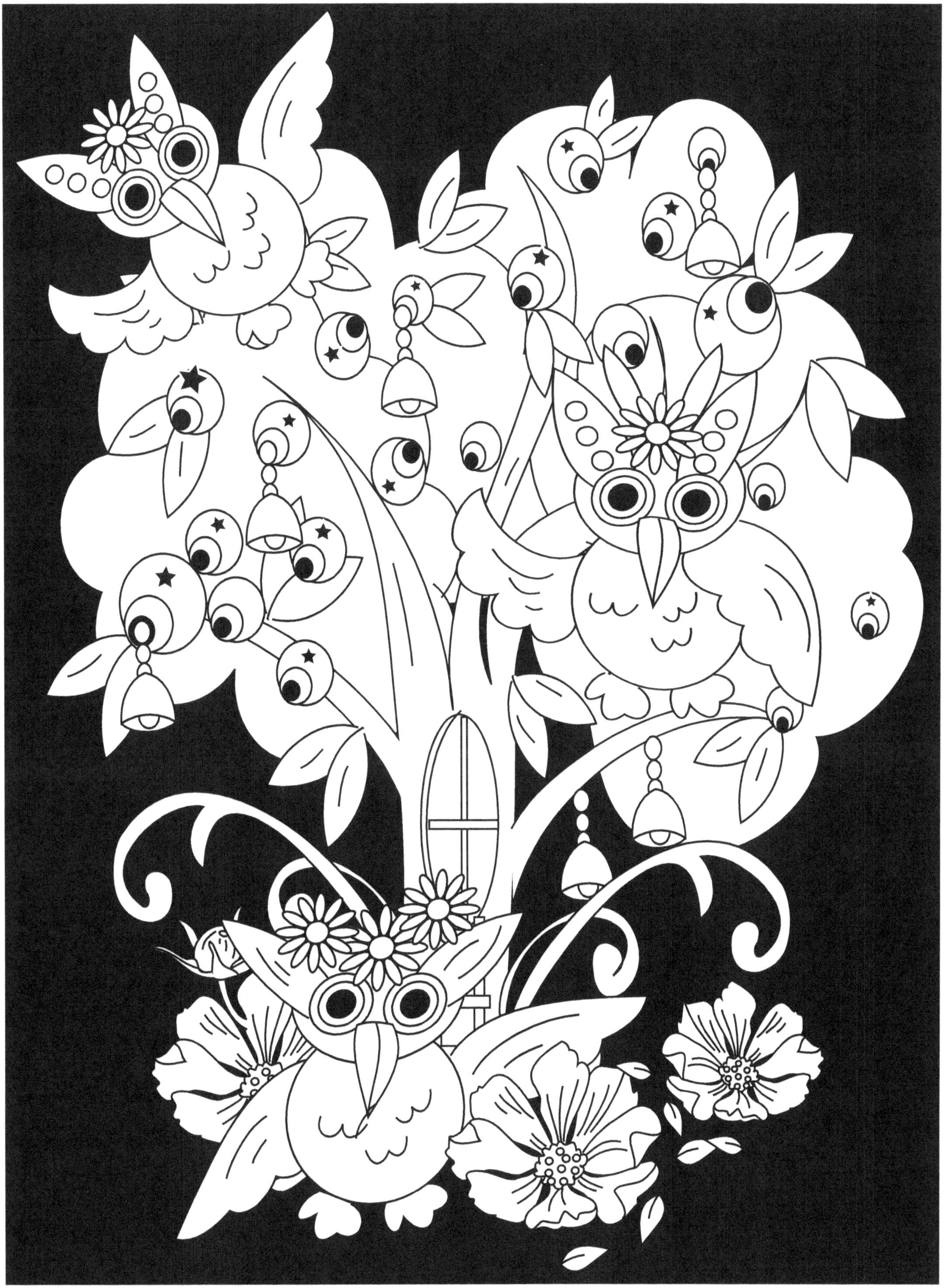

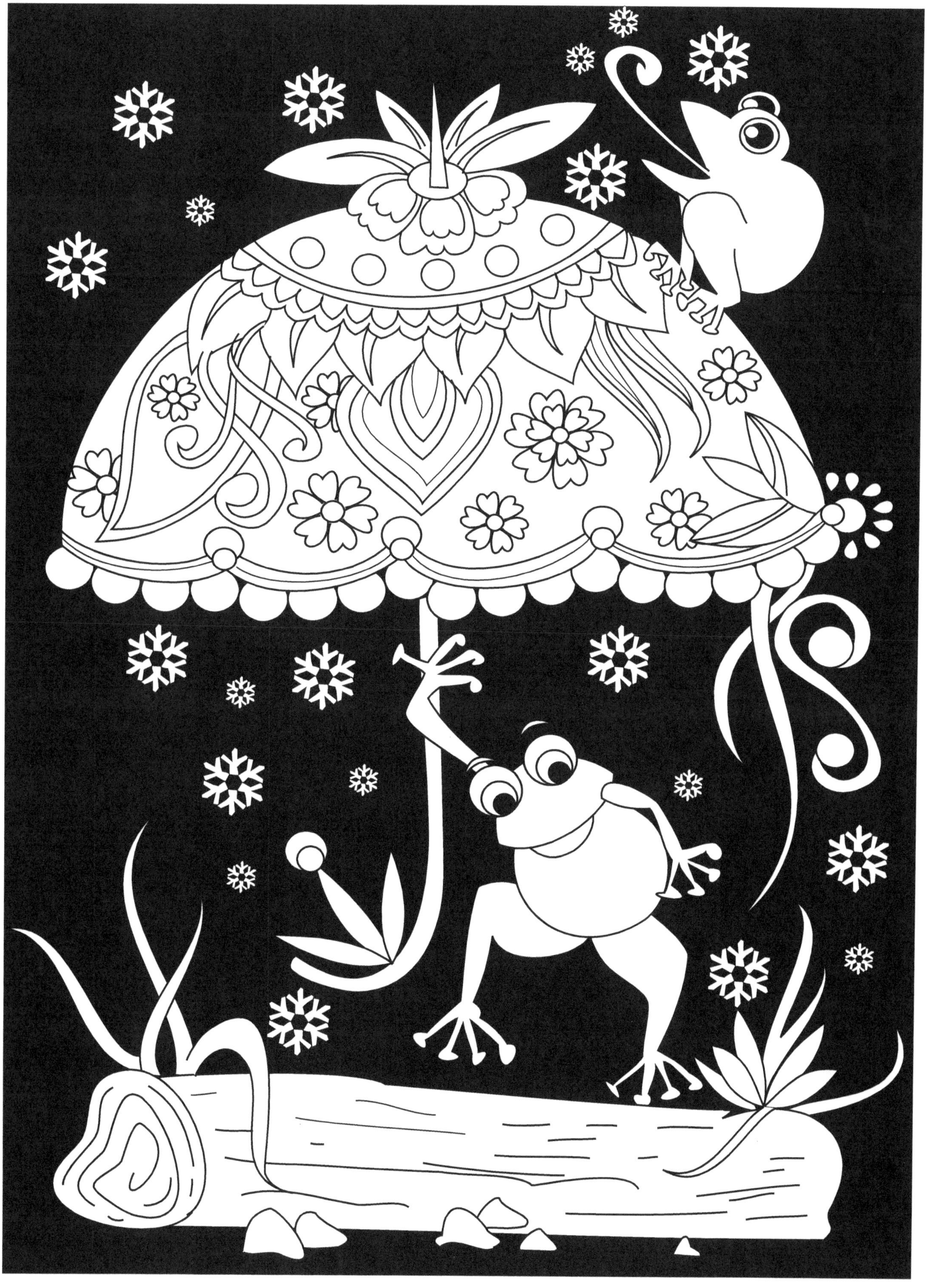

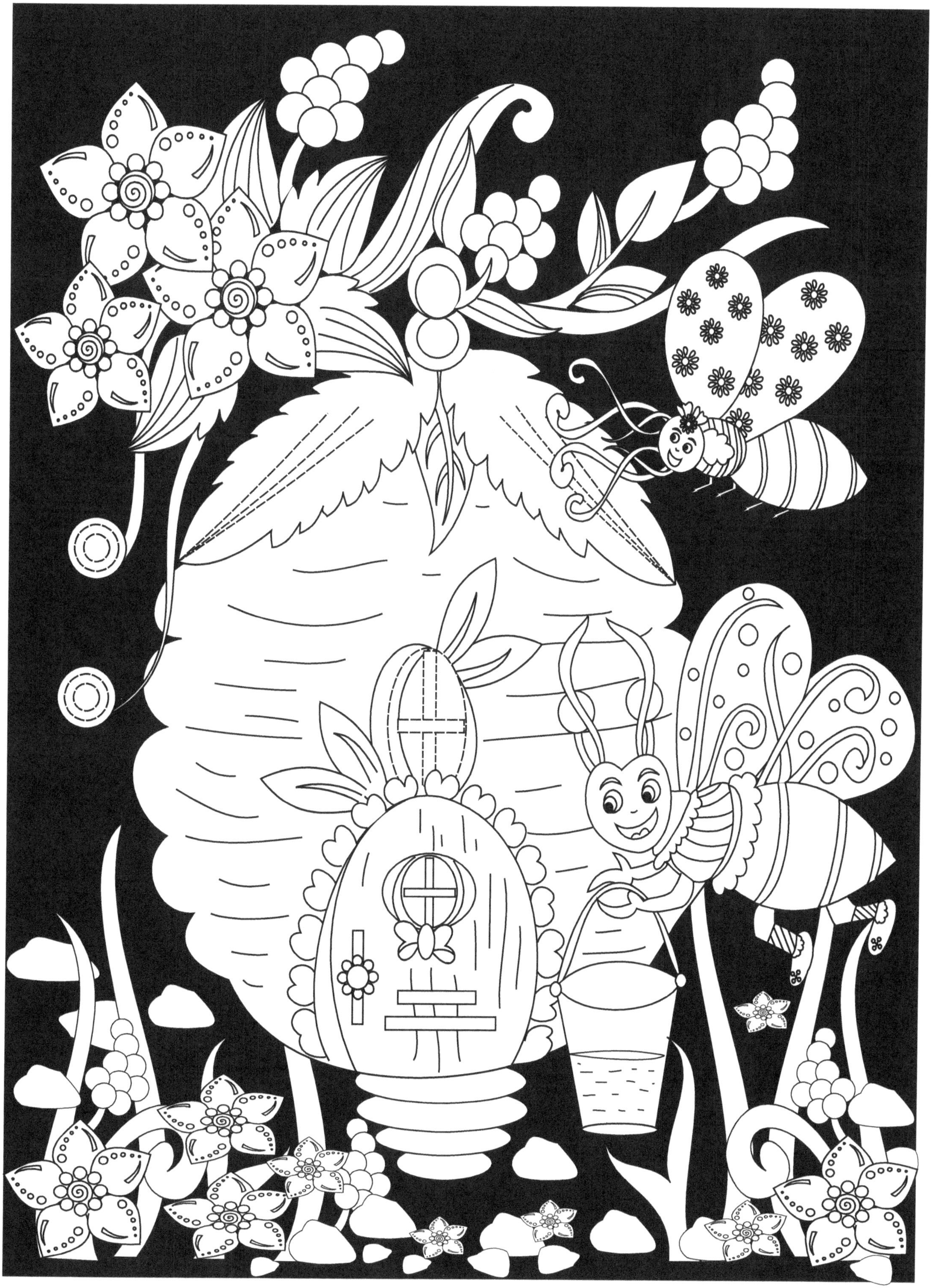

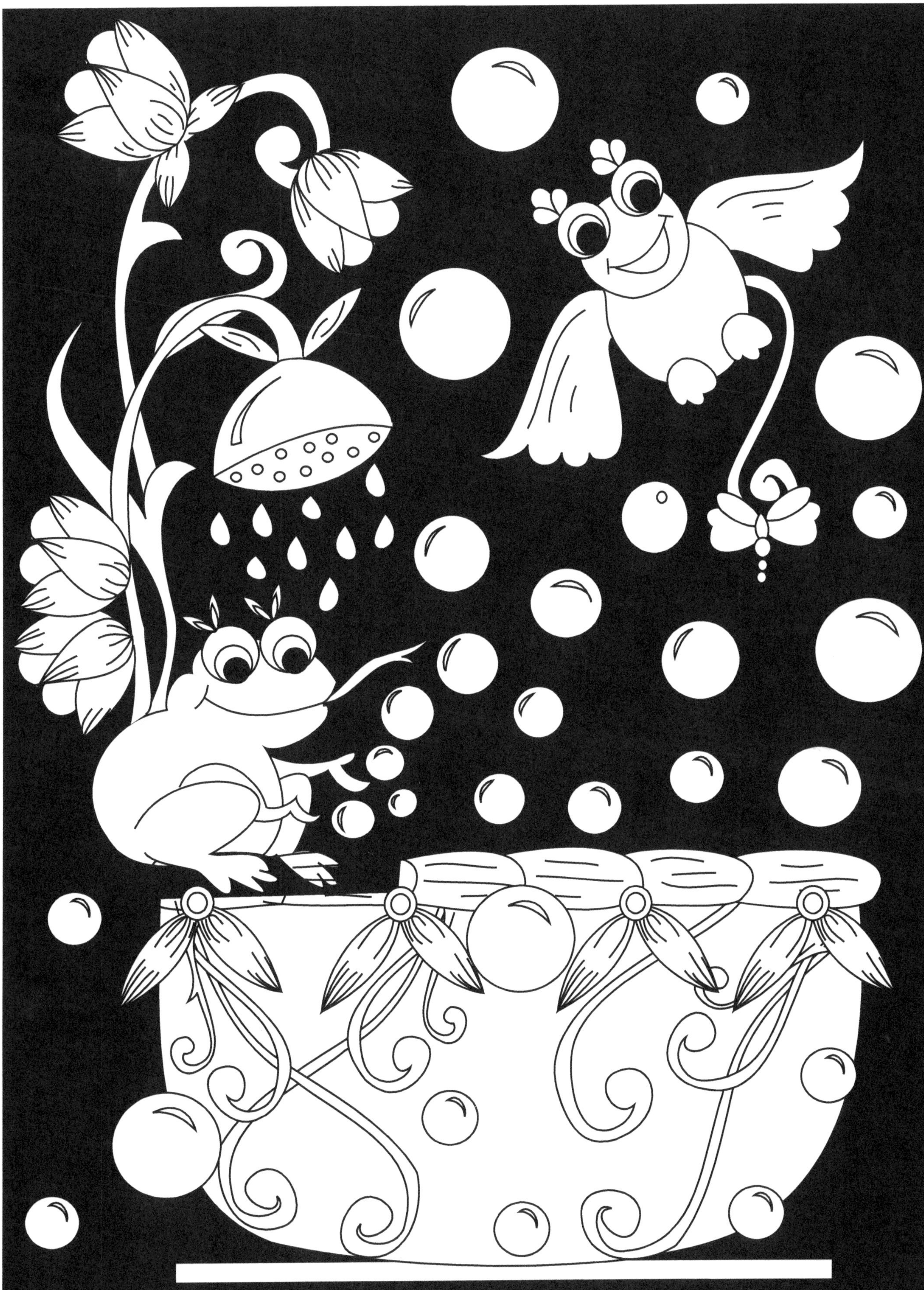

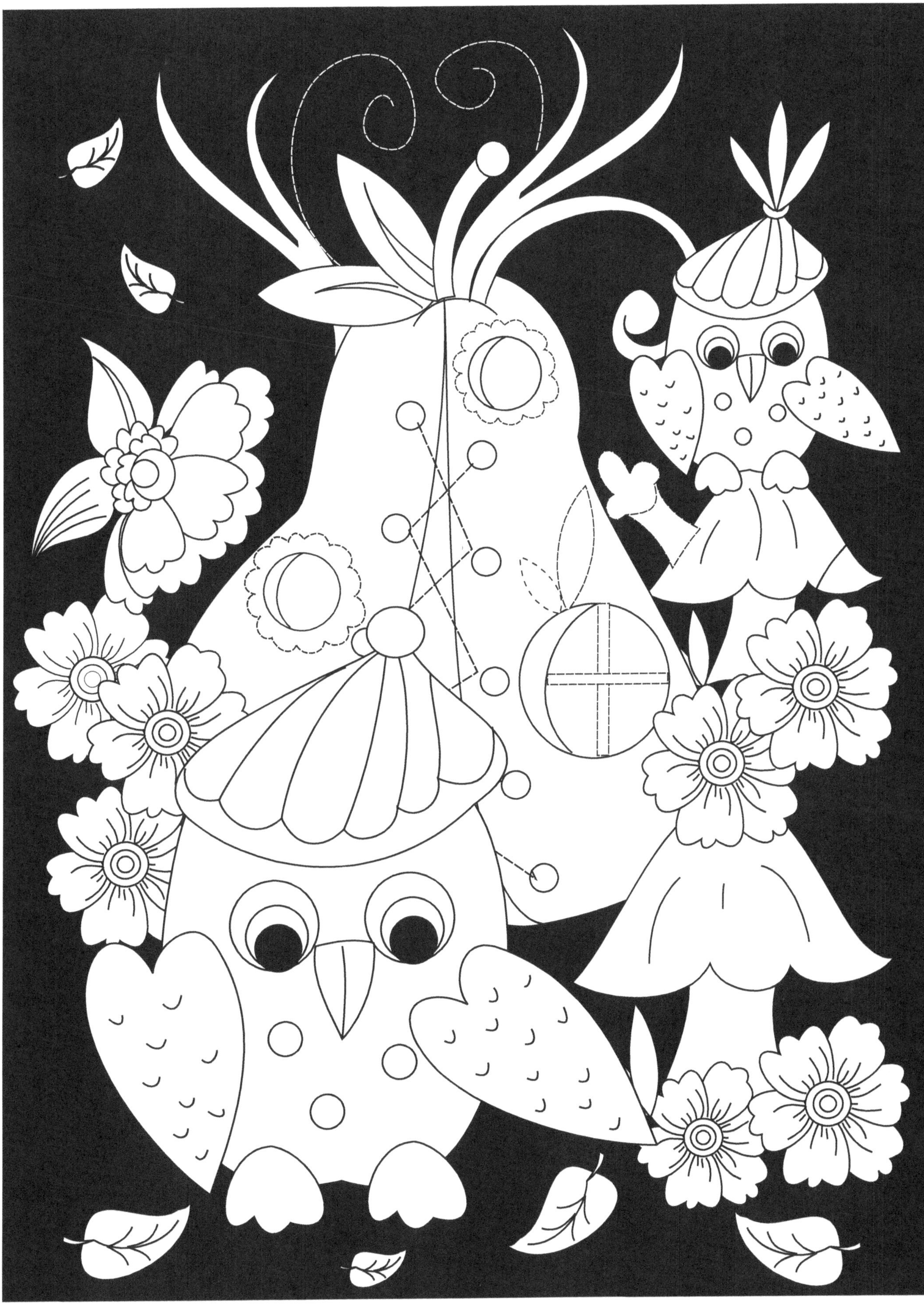

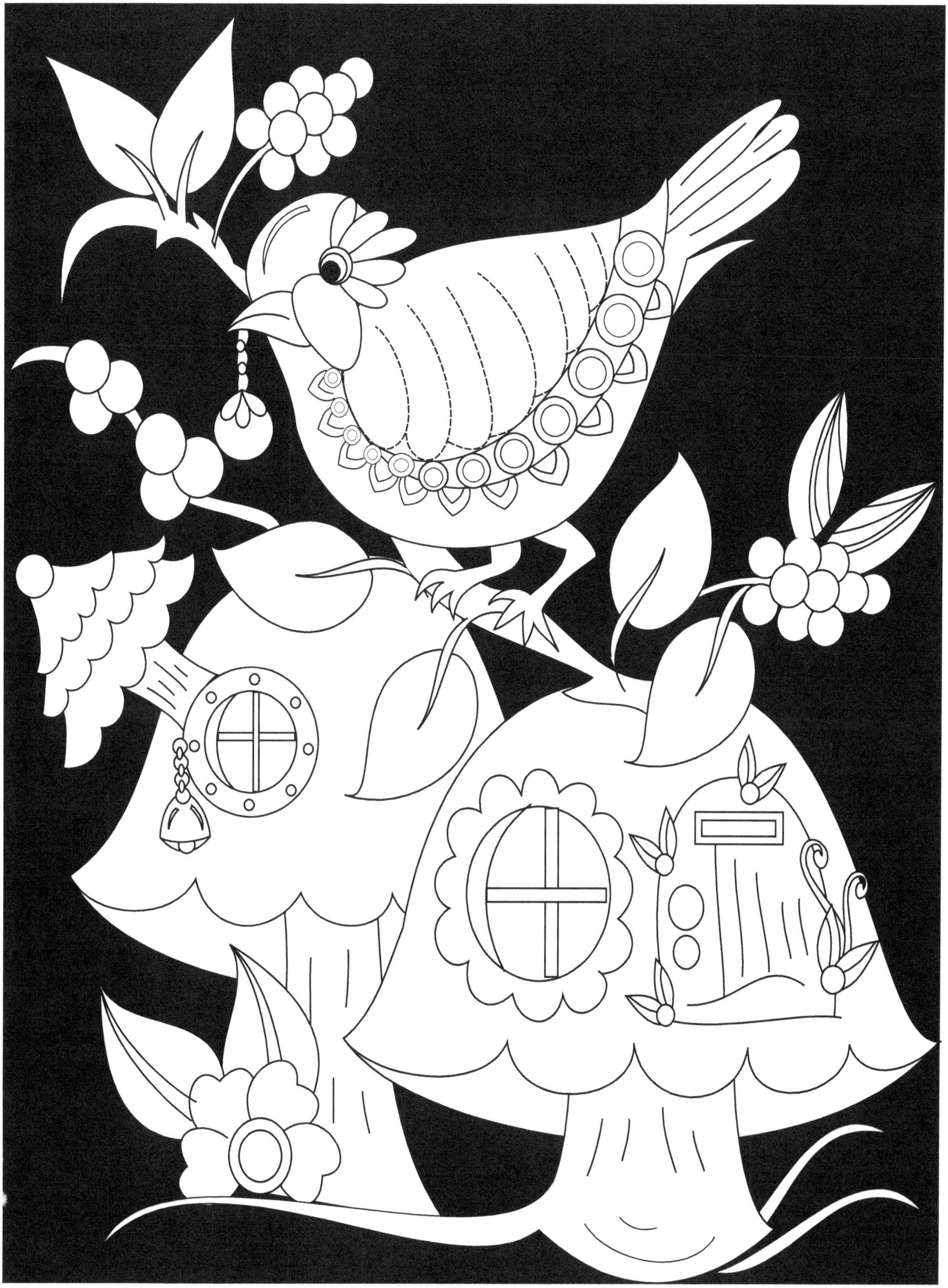

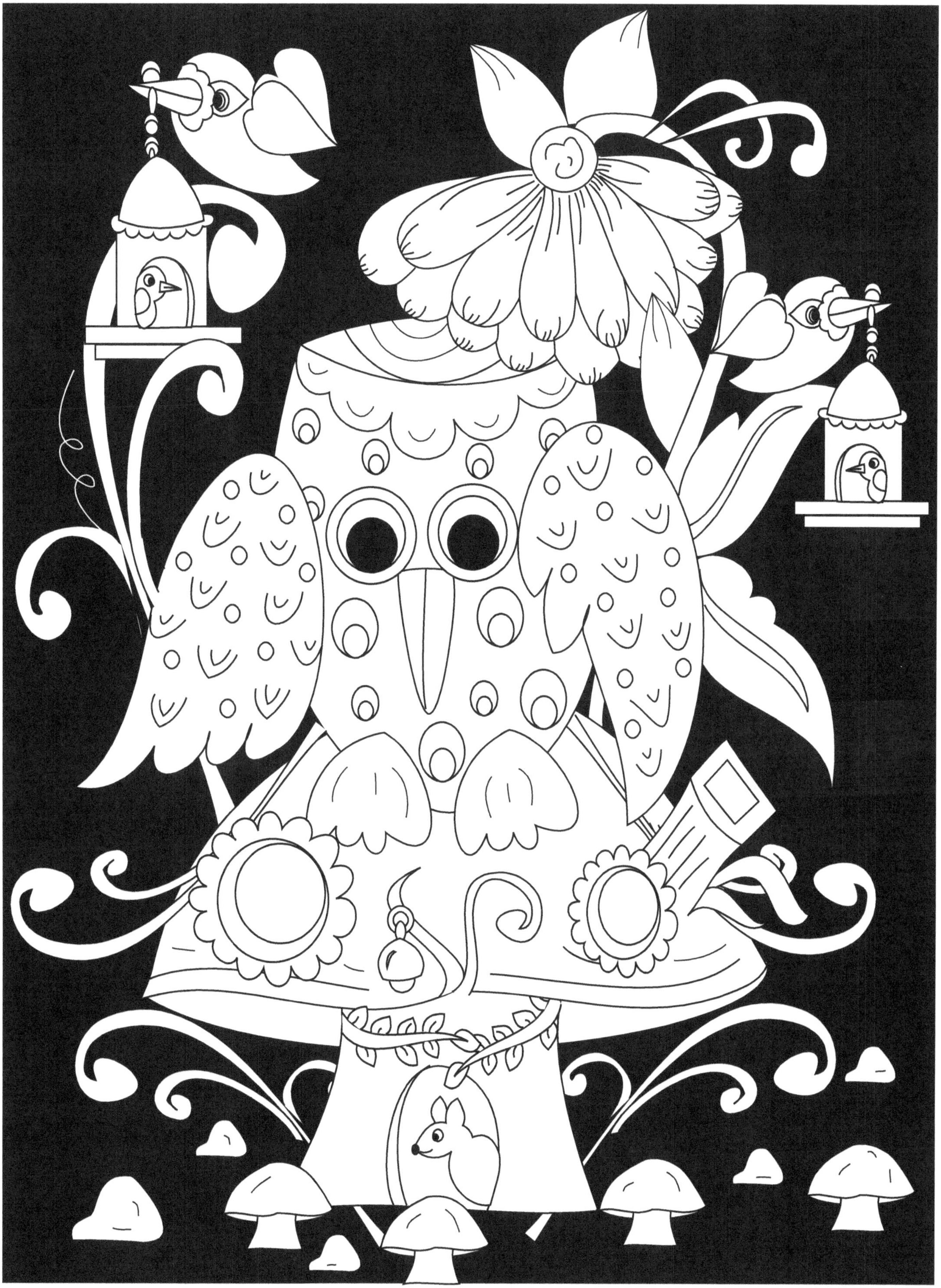

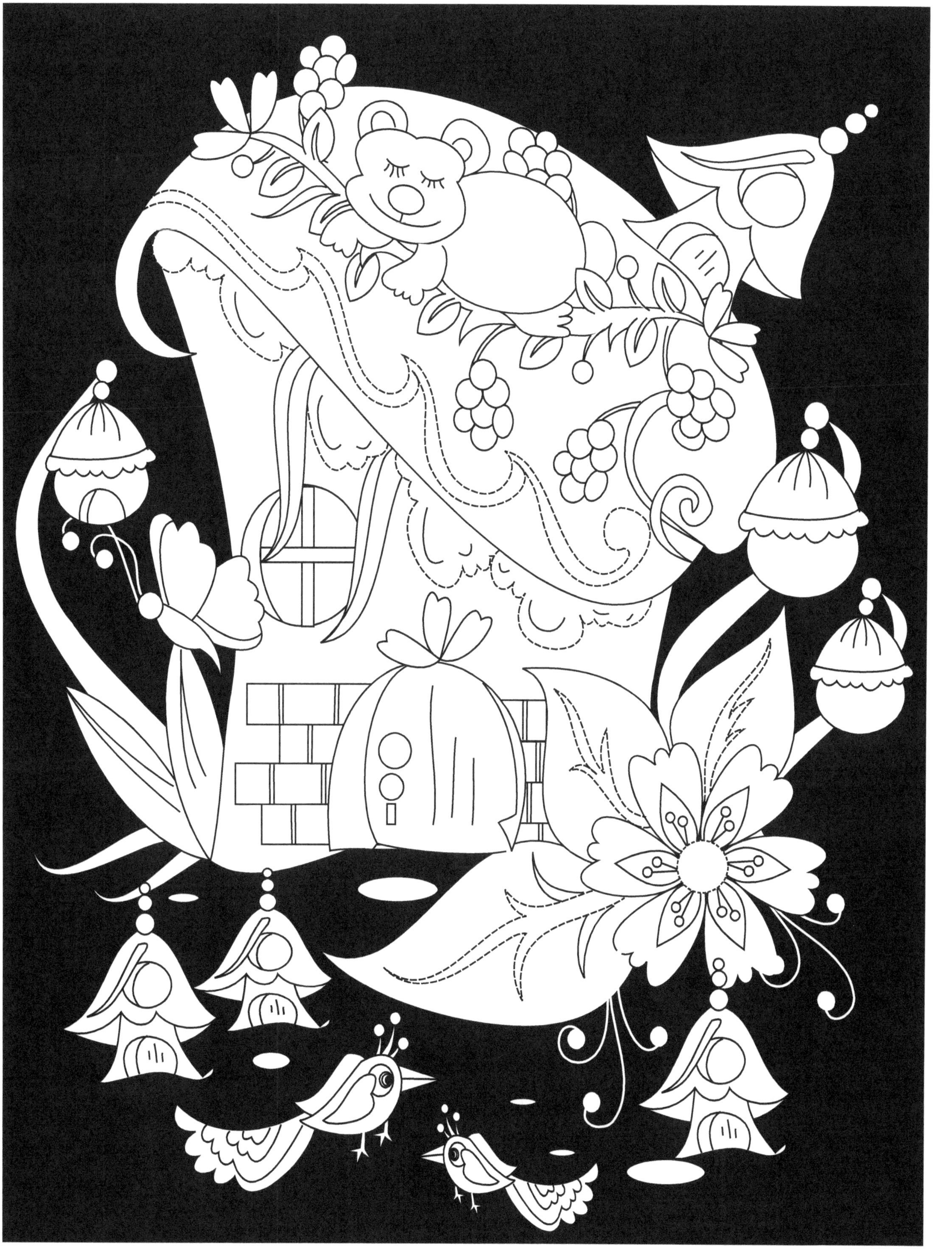

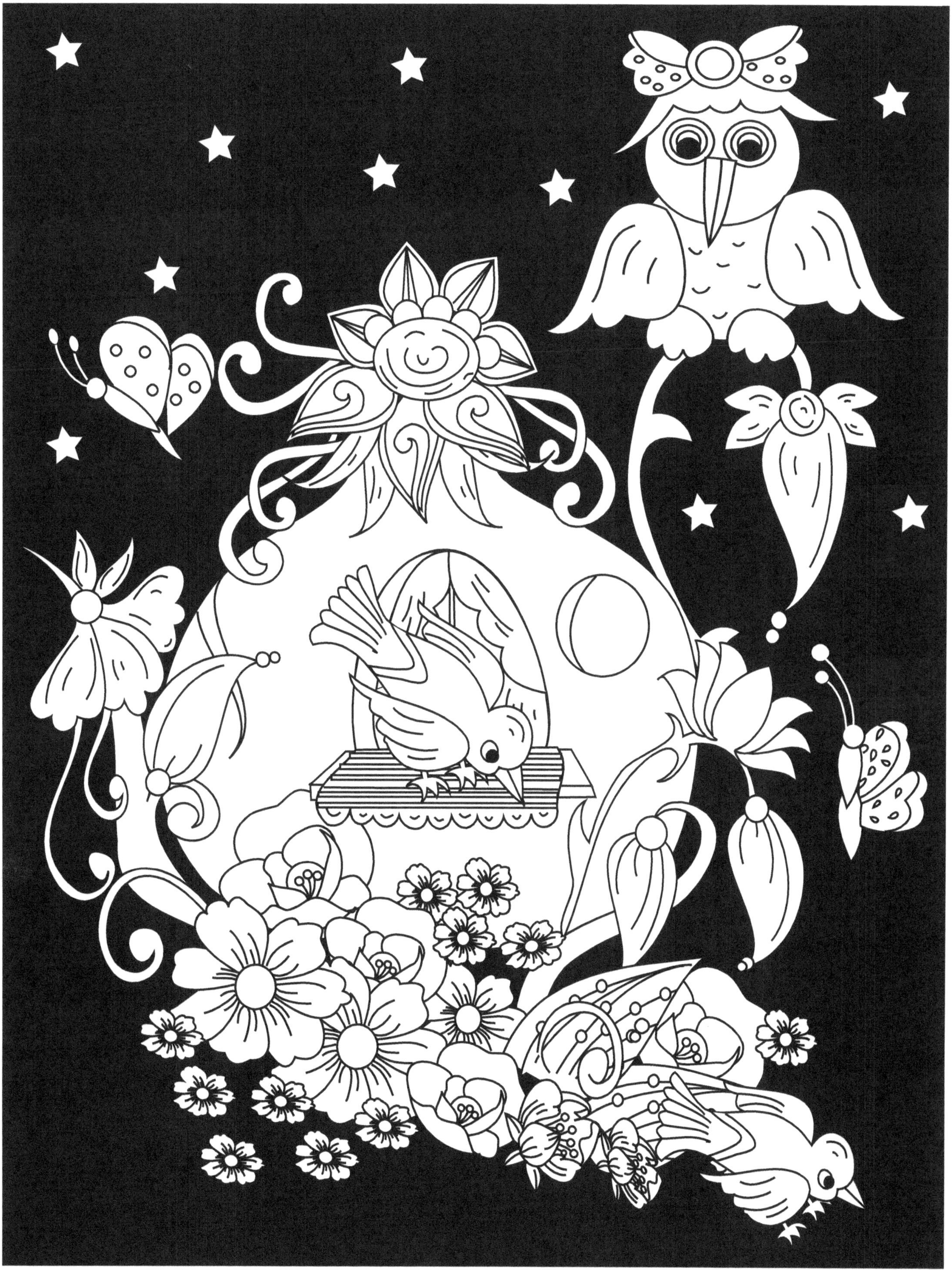

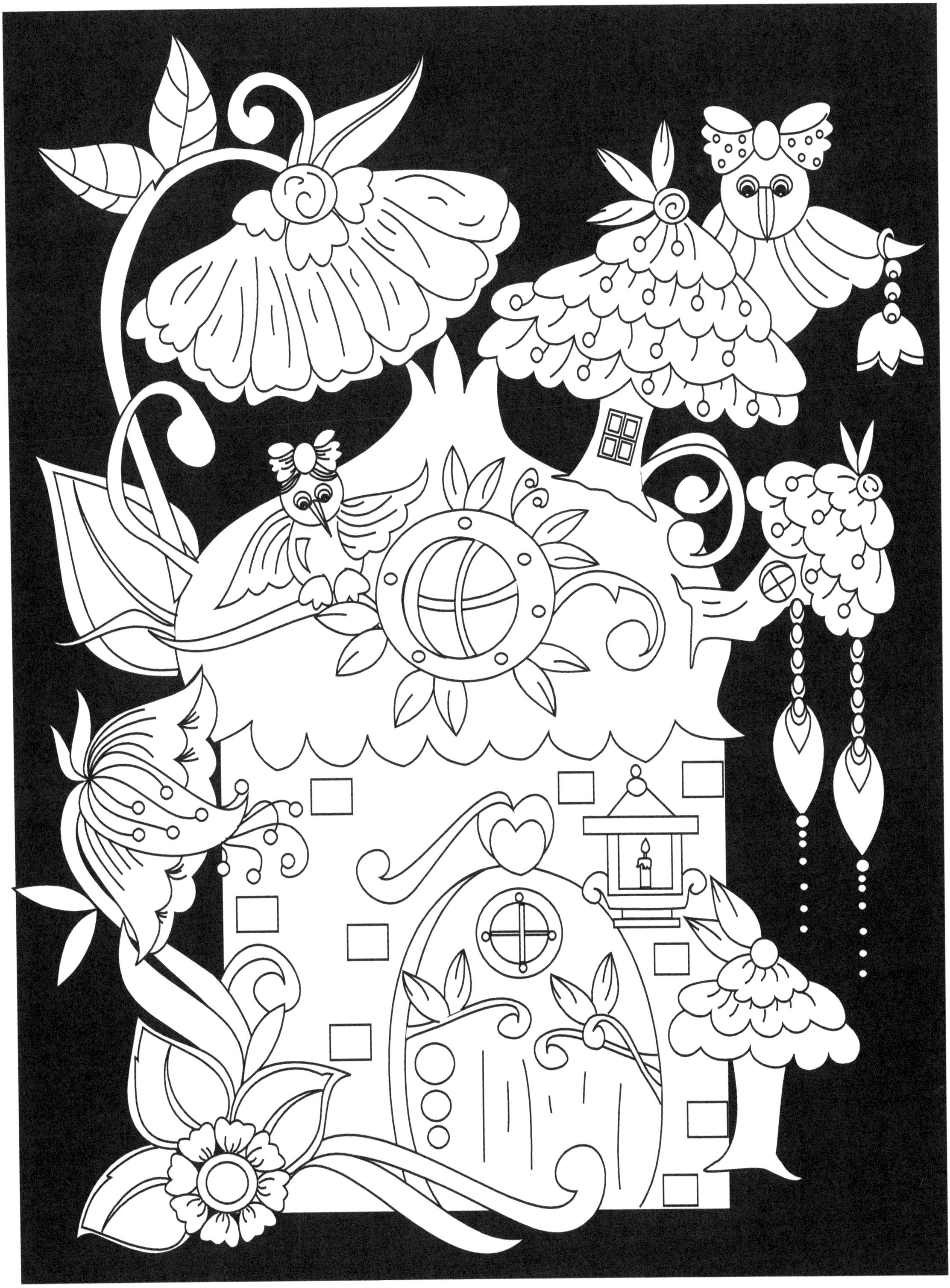

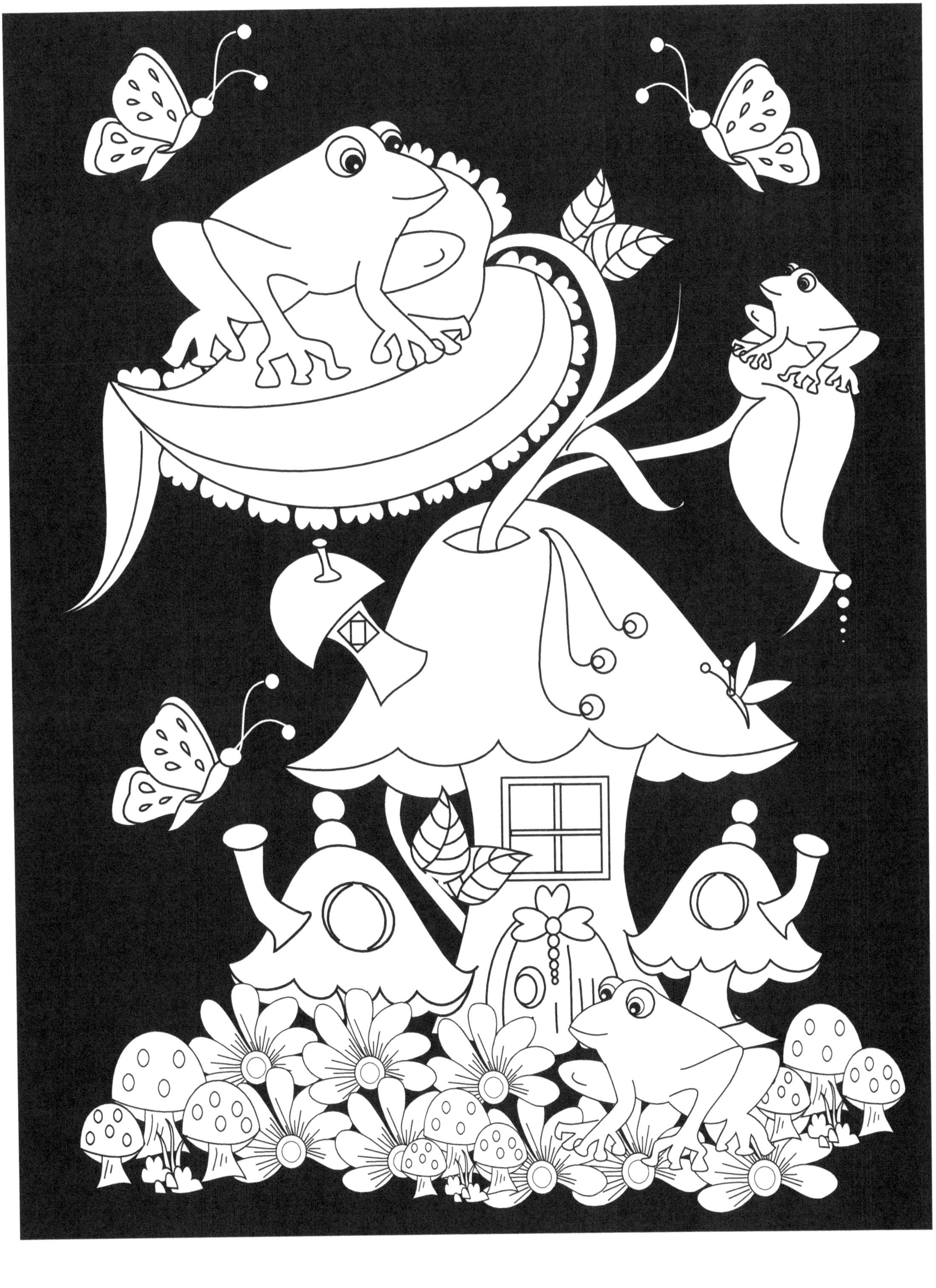

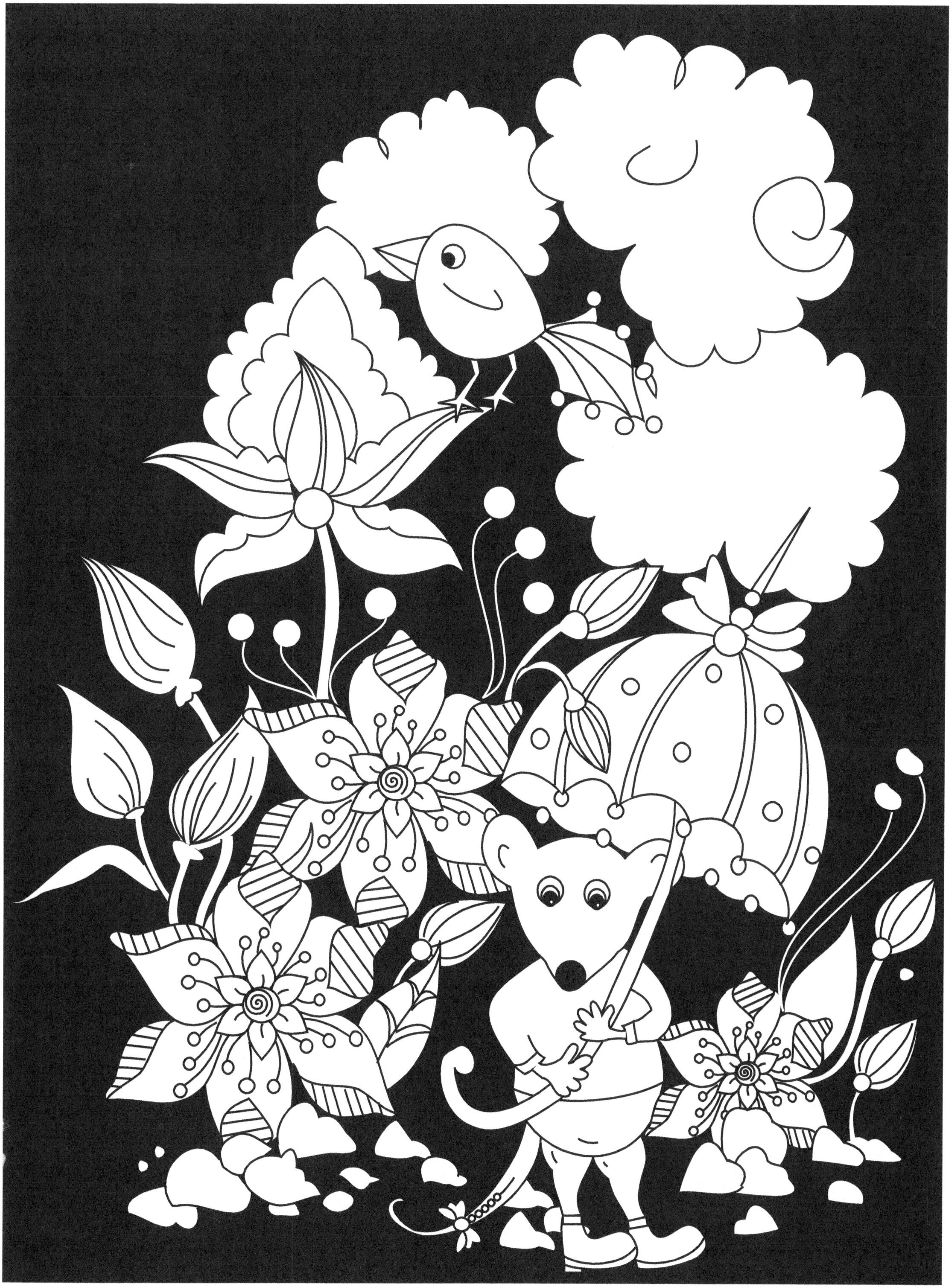

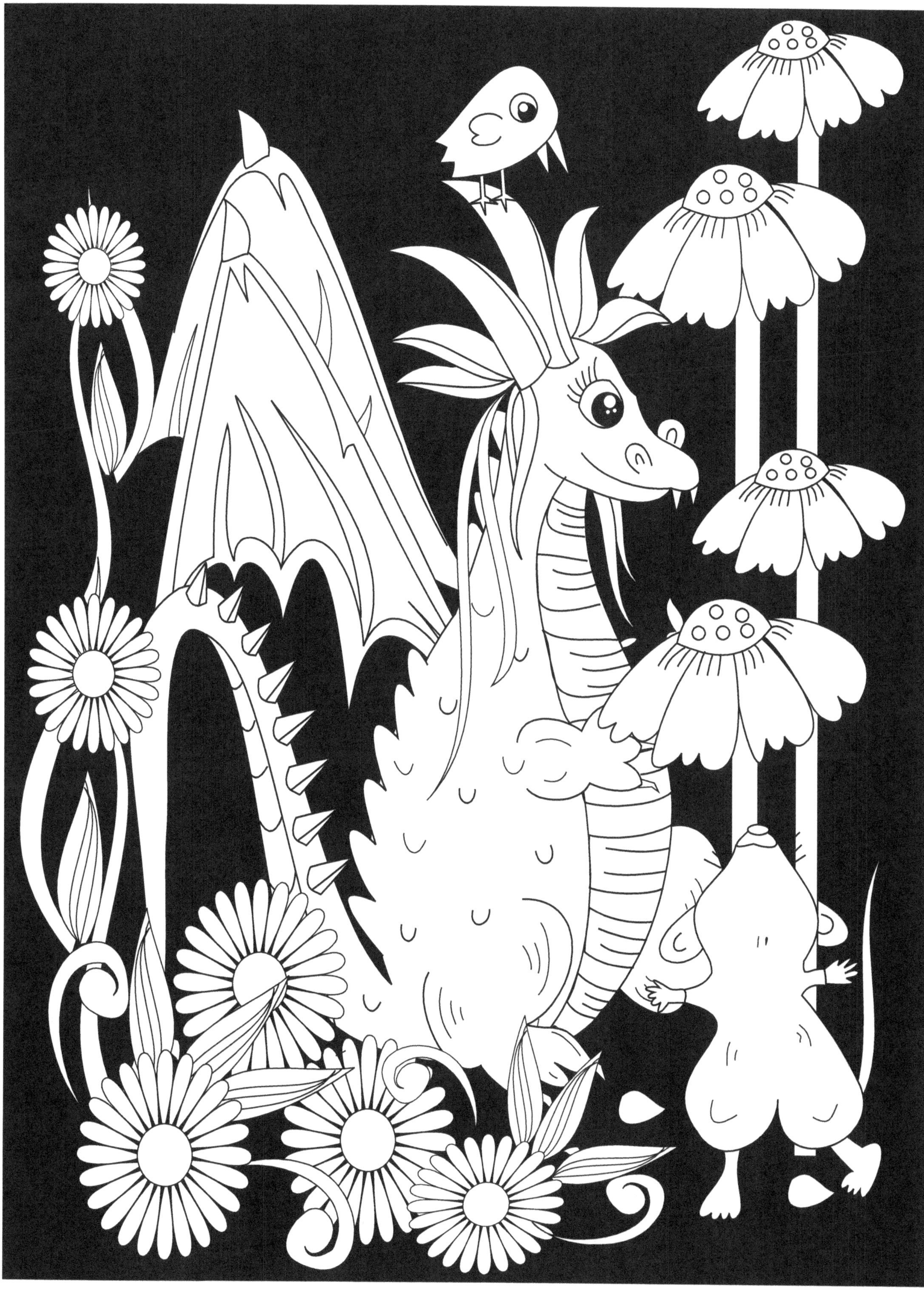

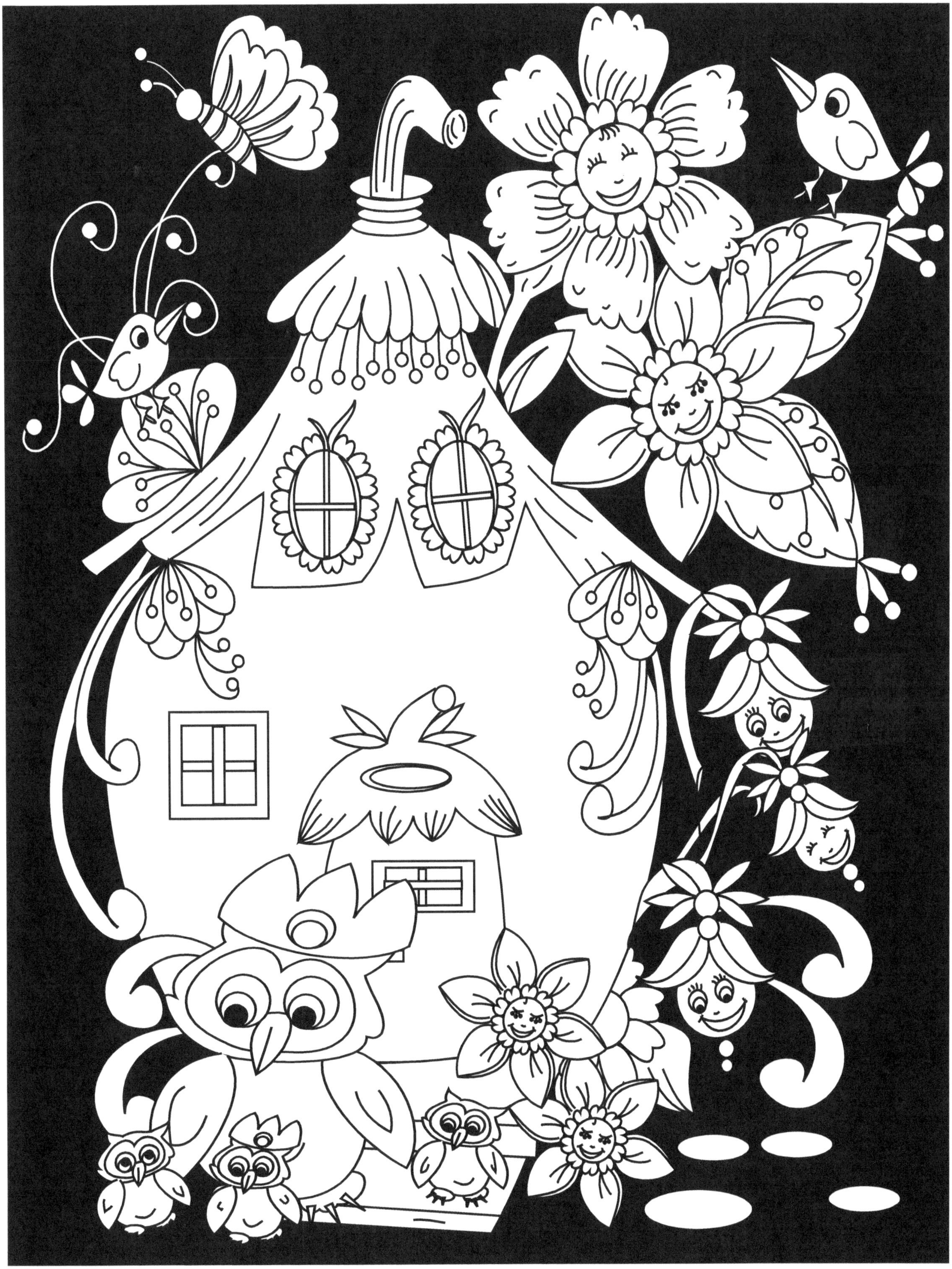

SWEET
HOME

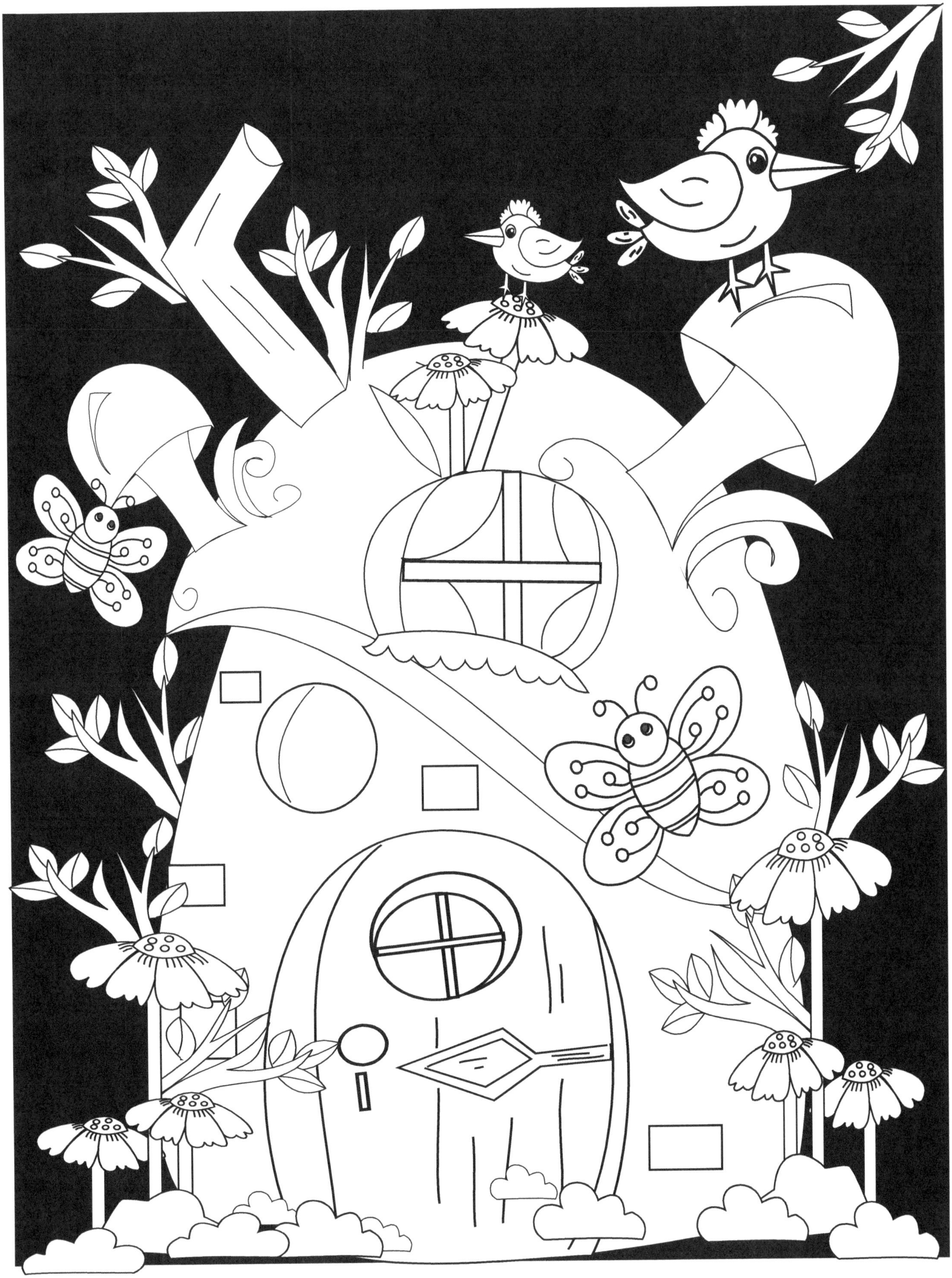

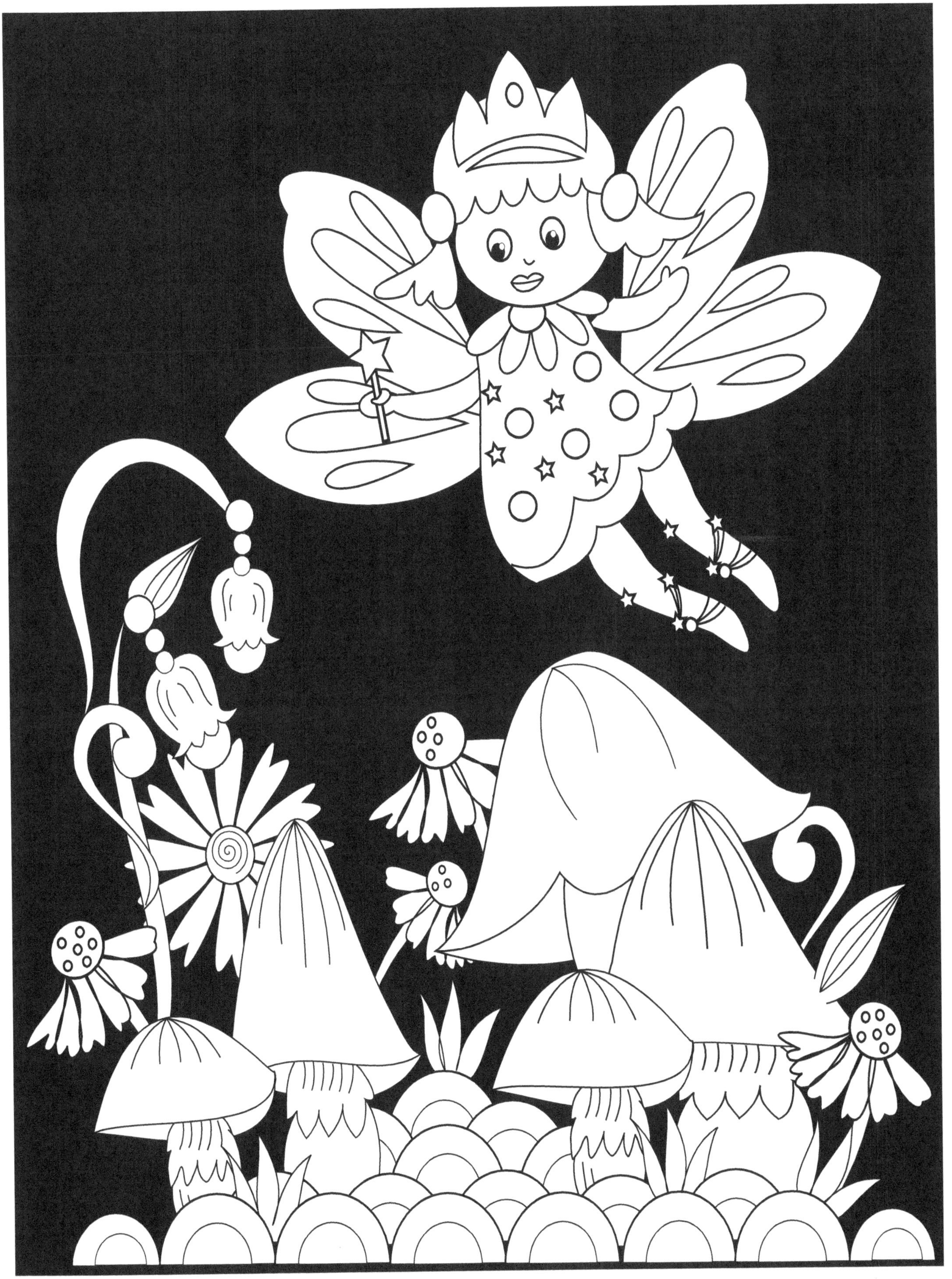

Color test

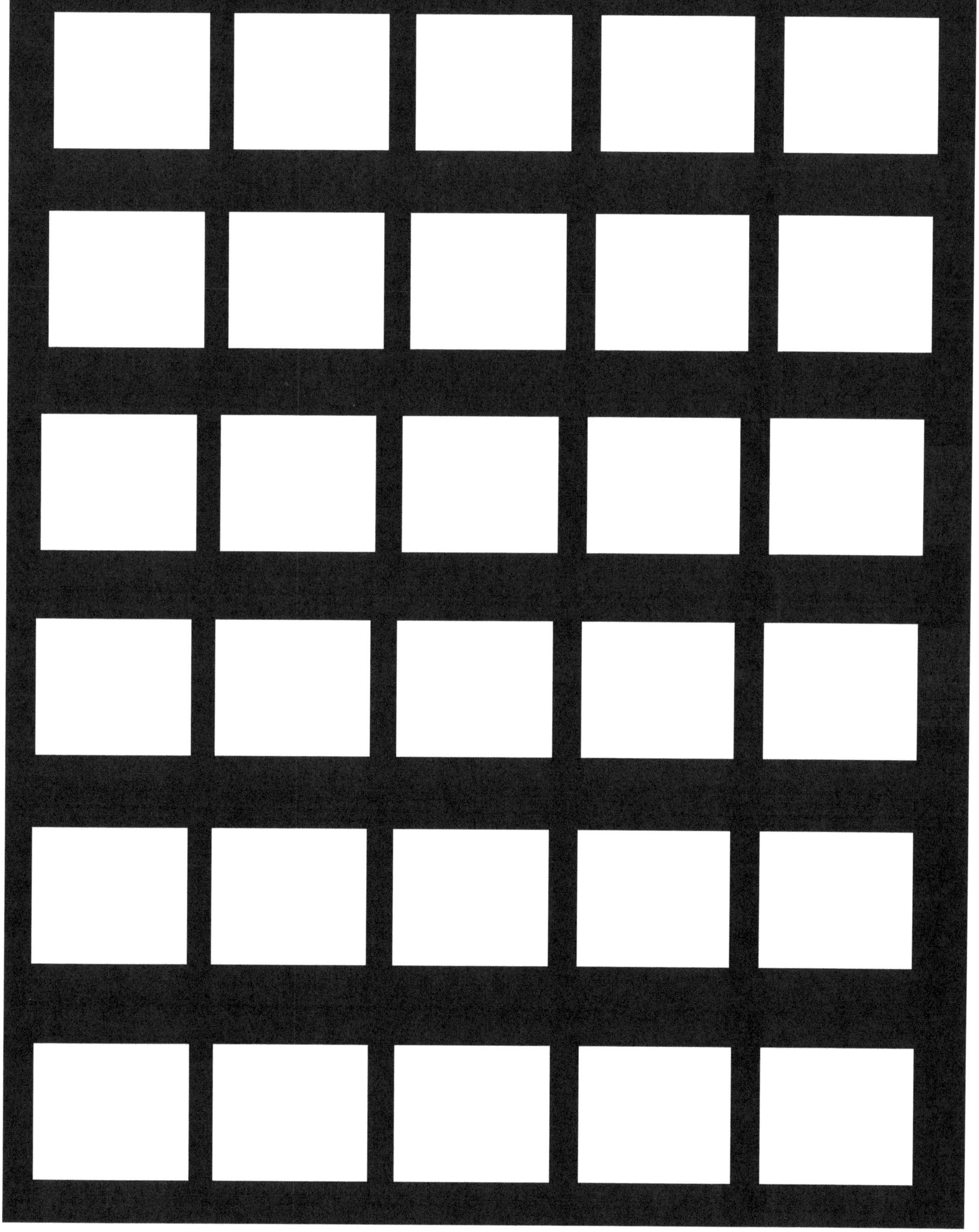

www.ingramcontent.com/pod-product-compliance
Lightning Source LLC
Chambersburg PA
CBHW080510220526
45465CB00006B/2430
* 9 7 9 8 6 2 1 7 8 0 7 9 1 *